Scholastic
Literacy
Skills

Spelling

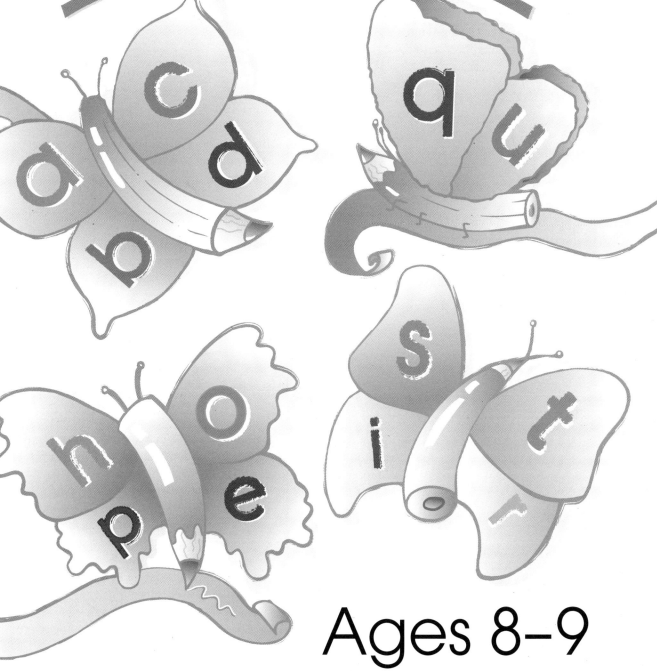

Ages 8–9

Photocopiable skills activities

Acknowledgements

Adapted from original material entitled *Spell Well* © Gordon Winch and Gregory Blaxell, published by Martin Education of Horwitz House, 55 Chandos St, St Leonards 2065, NSW, Australia.

The publishers gratefully acknowledge permission to reproduce the following copyright material:
(page 52) **Music Sales London Limited** for the first verse of *Ferry Cross The Mersey* by Gerry Marsden © 1964, Pacer Music Limited. Rights assigned 1976 Dick James Music Limited. All rights reserved. International Copyright Secured.
(pages 44 and 85) **Penguin Limited** for 'Scissors' and 'Picking Teams' from *Please Mrs Butler* by Allan Ahlberg © 1983, Allan Alhberg (1983, Penguin).

Every effort has been made to trace copyright holders and the publishers apologise for any inadvertent omissions.

Series consultant	Norma Mudd
Editor	Dulcie Booth
Assistant Editor	Clare Gallaher
Designer	Erik Ivens
Series designer	Paul Cheshire
Cover illustration	Lynda Murray

Designed using Adobe Pagemaker
Published by Scholastic Ltd, Villiers House, Clarendon Avenue, Leamington Spa, Warwickshire CV32 5PR
Printed by Ebenezer Baylis & Son Ltd, Worcester

© 1997, 2002 Scholastic Ltd

1 2 3 4 5 6 7 8 9   2 3 4 5 6 7 8 9 0 1

British Library Cataloguing-in-Publication Data
A catalogue record for this book is available from the British Library.

ISBN 0-439-98331-2

Contents

Supplementary units

Introduction

Scholastic Literacy Skills: Spelling is a structured spelling scheme for primary children from Years 3–6 (P4–7) and has been designed to meet children's spelling needs for these vital years of literacy development.

Good spelling is one of the most visible indications of literacy. It serves the purpose of good communication and marks the writer as one who has achieved a certain level of proficiency in literacy. It frees writers to concentrate more fully on the writing task itself. While it is important that children are given opportunities for 'free' writing, their ability to spell will not naturally improve if teaching only happens as and when individual needs arise.

Learning to spell is a developmental process and Scholastic Literacy Skills: Spelling focuses attention on the need for systematic teaching of spelling. An ongoing programme that involves the whole class in direct teaching is the best way to help children to become independent, effective spellers and fluent, confident writers. This is where Scholastic Literacy Skills: Spelling, with its unit-by-unit, context-based approach to learning and practising spellings, can help.

What should children know by the end of Year 2/P3?

Scholastic Literacy Skills: Spelling is developmentally structured to take children through the stages of spelling knowledge from Years 3–6 (P4–7). It is assumed that by the end of Year 2 (P3) children know all the letter names and sounds (especially the five vowels, and the use of the letter y as a vowel), both aurally and in written form. They should be able to form letters correctly and spell high-frequency words which observe common letter patterns (for example, can, dog, man). They should be able to spell some high-frequency but irregular words in terms of sight–sound correspondence (for example, the, my, we). The Dolch list of high-frequency words is given on page 23 and can be used (along with the National Literacy Strategy Framework for Teaching high- and medium-frequency words lists) as a quick assessment test of your class's spelling needs.

Spelling in the National Curriculum for England and Wales

Key Stage 1
Scholastic Literacy Skills: Spelling Ages 7–8 is aimed at the early stages of Key Stage 2, but it revises the following aspects of the National Curriculum for English. By the end of Key Stage 1, children should be able to:
- write each letter of the alphabet
- use their knowledge of sound–symbol relationships and phonological patterns
- recognise and use simple spelling patterns
- write common letter strings within familiar and common words
- spell commonly occurring simple words
- spell words with common prefixes and suffixes
- check the accuracy of their spelling, using wordbanks and dictionaries
- use their knowledge of word families and other words
- identify reasons for misspellings.

Key Stage 2

The National Curriculum for English at Key Stage 2 states that children should be taught:

- the meanings, uses and spellings of common prefixes and suffixes
- the spellings of words with inflectional endings
- the relevance of word families, roots and origins of words
- the use of appropriate terminology including *vowel, consonant, homophone* and *syllable.*

It also states that children should be taught the following spelling strategies:

- to sound out phonemes
- to analyse words into syllables and other known words
- to apply knowledge of spelling conventions
- to use knowledge of common letter strings, visual patterns and analogies
- to check their spelling using wordbanks, dictionaries and spellcheckers
- to revise and build on their knowledge of words and spelling patterns.

(from *The National Curriculum: Handbook for Primary Teachers in England* © Crown copyright 1999; © Qualifications and Curriculum Authority 1999)

Scholastic Literacy Skills: Spelling covers all the spelling strategies mentioned above. It introduces and explains rules, and provides opportunities for practice and revision. Using the Look–Say–Cover–Write–Check method of learning spellings, children learn to spell words and write them in personal wordbanks. They are encouraged to re-enter misspelled words into these wordbanks correctly. *Scholastic Literacy Skills: Spelling* introduces children to using a dictionary and gives practice in using a dictionary effectively (by direct teaching and regular practice). Children are also introduced to using an etymological dictionary and to using a thesaurus.

The 5–14 National Guidelines for Scotland

The 5–14 National Guidelines make specific reference to spelling in the English Language programmes of study: 'The teaching of spelling should be part of an agreed scheme… Supporting use should be made of a published spelling scheme graduated according to pupils' progress.' Explicit reference is made to the Look–Say–Cover–Write–Check strategy as being one method of teaching children to deal with mistakes. The 5–14 National Guidelines also make specific reference to the value of each child having a personal spelling book; this, in the form of the wordbank, is an important feature of *Scholastic Literacy Skills: Spelling.*

The Northern Ireland Curriculum

In discussing spelling within the context of the Writing Programme of Study, the Northern Ireland Curriculum outlines a broad progression at Key Stage 2 that reflects that built into *Scholastic Literacy Skills: Spelling* – 'from spelling common and familiar words in a recognisable way towards spelling more complex words correctly'. More specifically, it expects that at the end of Key Stage 2 children should be able to spell from memory frequently used words, to apply a variety of strategies to spell unfamiliar words and to use dictionaries and thesauruses. All these skills are addressed through *Scholastic Literacy Skills: Spelling.*

Common questions about spelling

Many teachers are unsure about how to teach spelling. Some common concerns are:
- How do I cope with varying levels of ability?
- How do I help children to look carefully at words so that they can recall them from memory and not just copy them 'thoughtlessly'?
- How do I help those children with specific difficulties in literacy-related areas?
- How do I encourage children to use dictionaries speedily and to locate the etymology of words?

Scholastic Literacy Skills: Spelling helps to answer these questions. It covers and continuously reviews all the areas of spelling required by the UK national curricula. Furthermore, it fulfils criteria for developing a holistic approach to literacy that links spelling, reading, writing, and speaking and listening.

A variety of strategies

Scholastic Literacy Skills: Spelling's approach to the teaching of spelling combines a variety of strategies based upon relevant research on how children learn to spell. These strategies include knowledge of:

1. Sound–symbol relationships

Much has been written about the irregularities in the English spelling system in terms of spelling according to the sounds we hear. In fact, the English writing system can be regarded as at least 80 per cent regular. Novice writers who spell according to sound (for example, *I haf a bic* for *I have a bike*) are able to communicate their message adequately, even if the spellings are incorrect.

It is, therefore, essential that children first learn the relationship between the names and the sounds of the 26 letters of the alphabet and also their appearance in graphic form. Later, children need to know the 44 sounds (or phonemes) in the English language (see page 22 for a list of the phonemes).

The research of Peter Bryant and Lynette Bradley, and Usha Goswami and Bryant, indicates that even very young children are usually sensitive to the sounds they hear. Children are particularly sensitive to rime (or what teachers may refer to approximately as rhyme) and onset (the first consonant/s in a word such as the *s* in *sing* and the *dr* in **dr**op).

Findings indicate that children who are helped to develop their phonological awareness and sense of rhyme at an early age are likely to learn to read and spell more easily. A knowledge of the aural aspects of the writing process is integral to the approach in *Scholastic Literacy Skills: Spelling*.

2. Blends and digraphs

Though many children can detect and identify sounds in words, problems sometimes arise when they try to write what they hear as they say a word. Words which cause difficulty are those with letters that blend or run together when they are spoken (for example, *sing, stop*) or with two letters that have only one sound (these are called digraphs, of which *ea, ai, ch, ck, sh* are examples). *Scholastic Literacy Skills: Spelling* practises and revises common blends and digraphs, and encourages children to read texts aloud, listening for certain sounds while they look at the corresponding written form. This focus on careful listening and looking is a vital strategy in improving children's awareness of the 'trickier' aspects of the English spelling system.

3. Pronunciation of words

Teachers and parents can help children to spell by articulating words clearly and correctly and, when necessary, by drawing their attention to how a particular sound is voiced. It is even more helpful to show children how a particularly tricky sound looks in writing. Often, if children want to represent a sound when they are spelling a word, but have difficulty in finding a perfect fit, they will choose a near fit by using a letter that approximates to the sound they wish to represent. For example, children who have difficulty with the *th* digraph may say (and then write) *free* for *th*ree, or *tay/tey* for *th*ey. Similarly, it is common for some children to omit the *h* from *wh* words (for example, *wh*isper, *wh*en, *wh*ere). Some misspellings may be caused by difficulties in discriminating some sounds (see 'Helping children with spelling difficulties', page 18). Throughout *Scholastic Literacy Skills: Spelling*, children read texts aloud to themselves and/or others. Teachers may decide to read some texts aloud to the class, to model clear, correct pronunciation; this may differ according to regional accents so that, for example, the *u* sound in *book* may be pronounced as *oo*, especially in parts of Northern England.

4. Syllabification

The strategy of dividing words into syllables is helpful in several ways. It enables children to remember how to spell longer words by finding shorter, known words or roots within the longer word (for example, *know* and *edge* in *knowledge*). It can help them not to omit parts of longer words (for example, *en vi ron ment* or *dis app ear*) by focusing on short sound units (there are far fewer syllables than there are letters in the words). This strategy also reinforces correct pronunciation of words. Syllabification is a regular feature of activities in *Scholastic Literacy Skills: Spelling*.

5. Sight–symbol relationships

As novice spellers progress from the phonetic stage of spelling, they become increasingly aware that letter sounds do not always have a constant representation in writing. For example, the *as* in the word *was* is often written by novice spellers as *woz*. Such spellers begin to rely more on visual and morphemic (or meaning-bearing) clues, and need to pay special attention to the visual aspects of words. They need to work on developing a visual memory, locating difficult parts of words by looking carefully at tricky spellings. The ability to look carefully at words needs thoughtful and explicit teaching. In normal reading, it is possible to make sense of text while paying minimal attention to the spelling of individual words. A good visual memory is best achieved (especially for tricky words, for example those with irregular sound–symbol correspondences) by using the Look–Say–Cover–Write–Check method. Writers should then use the tricky words in the course of their own writing, or the words should form part of a contextualised writing activity.

6. Roots of words

Roots are the 'meaning-bearing chunks' of words. If learner spellers can identify roots, they can make sense of the fairly regular patterns of changes of meaning and spelling that occur when prefixes or suffixes are added to roots. They can then learn to build words and, conversely, to break them up to facilitate spelling, as explained in section 4 on the previous page.

7. Prefixes and suffixes from other languages

Prefixes and suffixes, when added to the root of a word, alter the meaning of the word. Many are of Latin or Greek origin. The earlier children are introduced to prefixes and suffixes, the better, as learning about them helps children to understand the meanings of new words, and consequently to spell them.

8. Word families

Independent, self-sufficient spelling should be the aim of every learner speller. A knowledge of word families (or word patterns) helps children to spell by analogy and to make an intelligent 'guess' at a spelling. It is important that children always 'have a go' at a spelling, so long as they then remember to check their guess. Word families are useful as a memory aid – the words can be put into a sentence to be learned, for example *I ought to have brought my books – I thought I had!* or *My friend has a piece of pie.* Encourage children to make up their own mnemonic sentences for words they find difficult. They could also collect new words for word families.

9. Kinaesthetic approaches

Kinaesthetic refers to the shape of a word. Kinaesthetic strategies, which involve using 3-D letters or letter shapes for children to move around to make words, or tracing over letters, are often recommended for children who experience difficulties with reading and spelling. In fact, many learner spellers benefit from this approach. The use of something tangible (for example, plastic letters or tracing in sand) can help make a learning task less abstract and transitory. For older learners, Scrabble tiles are an 'adult' version of the same approach.

10. Generalisations about the English spelling system

Many of the so-called 'rules' of spelling have exceptions to them. But if they are taught as generalisations with exceptions, they can provide a degree of security. *Scholastic Literacy Skills: Spelling* gives, practises and revises such rules in order to reduce the learning load.

Using *Scholastic Literacy Skills: Spelling*

Scholastic Literacy Skills: Spelling recognises that spelling is an integral part of the writing process, which includes grammar and punctuation, and requires an active approach so that children use and apply spellings in their reading and writing in all learning areas. It has been shown that learning spellings in isolation is not an effective way of ensuring this integration. *Scholastic Literacy Skills: Spelling* encourages children to work at improving their spelling in different contexts, giving relevance to the spelling task. It includes lively rhymes, poems, puzzles, jokes, short stories and information texts which hold children's attention, foster discussion and close engagement with texts. This approach gives real opportunities to both extend children's knowledge and to show them that learning to spell can be fun.

The four books in the series provide continuity, progression and flexibility for all the children in a class and are not merely collections of lists of words to be tested weekly. The supplementary photocopiable sheets in each book allow teachers to differentiate tasks even more finely, tailoring the units to suit individual needs.

General approaches

Scholastic Literacy Skills: Spelling is designed to be used flexibly in the classroom. Teachers will decide which approaches best suit their children. Some general approaches are:

Whole-class approach

If each child has a copy of the same unit, the spelling needs of the children can be met through progress as a class. This allows the whole class to work simultaneously on a shared text.

Group approach

This approach enables different-ability groups to work on different units. *Scholastic Literacy Skills: Spelling* caters for sequential development so that each photocopiable book dovetails into the next. This provides opportunities for flexible planning of a spelling programme. Exercises can be related to ongoing class work and/or projects. So, for example, when adjectives and nouns are discussed, it might be helpful to look at *Spelling Ages 8–9* (pages 70–1); or if word origins are discussed, the units on etymology in *Spelling Ages 9–10* (pages 64–5 and 92–3) could be used.

Skills-focus approach

Scholastic Literacy Skills: Spelling permits a systematic development of spelling skills suited to the different linguistic levels of children. In a class of eight- to nine-year-olds, for example, children of average ability in spelling (which may be most of the class) may work on units from *Spelling Ages 8–9*, while more able spellers work on units from *Spelling Ages 9–10*. Children who find spelling difficult may work on units from *Spelling Ages 7–8*, using the supplementary photocopiable pages to reinforce learning.

Teachers could spend between five and ten minutes explaining work to the 'average' spellers, while the less able spellers could be paired to test each other on spellings entered in their wordbanks. More able spellers could begin working unaided (initially). This helps children become accustomed to following instructions independently. After the first five or ten minutes, teachers will be available to give time to the less able spellers, explaining tasks carefully, checking their self-tests or revising recently learned work.

Using the units

Teachers can read instructions, poems and texts both to and with the children, especially less able spellers and readers. This is particularly recommended when using units from the books for *Spelling Ages 7–8* and *Spelling Ages 8–9*.

Make sure that children become familiar with the technical vocabulary used in the units (for example, *underline, complete, fill in, consonant, vowel (long* and *short), singular, plural* and so on). Don't forget that some children have difficulties in distinguishing left from right.

Ensure that children understand fully the Look–Say–Cover–Write–Check method of learning spellings. Encourage them to look carefully and to identify and underline tricky words or parts of words. Many novice spellers simply glance at a word to be learned without noting the shape of the individual letters. Model this strategy explicitly and often. Remind children regularly of the strategy when undertaking written work.

Effective proof-reading also requires modelling. The checking of work needs to be done quite slowly, word by word, if errors are to be detected. Making up mnemonics is something children enjoy, but remind them that their purpose is to remember how to spell a word. For example, if the sentence *The bus is busy* is used to aid the spelling of *bus*, then it should be explained that *busy* contains the word *bus*; this part of the word should be underlined.

Wordbanks

A photocopiable wordbank is provided on pages 100–2. It lists every word taught in the main units of this book, and has alphabetical headings so that children can have practice in developing skills using alphabetical order.

Setting up children's individual wordbanks is also important and children should be encouraged to use theirs as a quick reference for all written work. This should become a matter of instinct for children, but in the early stages regular use needs to be encouraged. Some children may be reluctant to re-enter words they misspell. It is, however, vital that they do re-enter words (particularly high-frequency words) that cause them difficulty. Each child and teacher will then be able to flick through the wordbank and quickly identify tricky words. For example, if *because* is entered three or four times, this indicates that the word needs specific attention.

Targeting tricky words

In the course of working on the activities, children are asked to make up their own sentences using target words. Encourage children to use words they have learned but found tricky. This means they will constantly revise high-frequency words that they find difficult. For example, if two of the words appearing several times in a child's wordbank are *because* and *should*, and an exercise asks for original sentences using words ending in *tion*, the child may write: *He **should** go to the sta**tion because** his friend is coming by train.*

Review units

The review units, which occur after every five units in the main section of the book, provide records of individual progress and highlight difficulties. Pairs of children can use the pages to test each other. Discuss progress with individual children, noting any difficulties that need specific attention.

Make sure children understand each part of the Look–Say–Cover–Write–Check method of learning spellings. It is important that they look carefully at the words to improve their visual memory. Saying the words helps them to associate the sounds with the visual appearance of the letters. Writing the words helps them to 'feel' the shape of the letters through the hand, especially if joined-up handwriting is encouraged from an early age. They must understand how and why to check their written work, using their wordbank or a dictionary to confirm that either their spellings are correct or that further practice may be needed.

Involving parents

Parents can give vital help, support and encouragement to their children as they progress towards becoming effective spellers. If parents are to support their children positively so that spellings are regarded as part of the wider writing process and not simply a list of unconnected words, they need to be made aware of the school's approach to teaching and improving spelling. Invite parents who are willing to help their children with their written work into school and talk through the school's philosophy and strategies for teaching writing and spelling.

Encourage parents to:
● take an interest in their child's writing at home. They should read it and give relevant praise for effort and content. They should avoid commenting firstly (or worse still only) on spelling errors, presentation and handwriting.
● involve their child in 'real' writing tasks, such as shopping lists, invitations, letters and notes to friends and relatives, diary entries and similar activities.
● help their child to 'edit' their written work and encourage the use of wordbanks and/or dictionaries to check spellings.
● have spelling games for fun – in the car, around the table, at bedtime.
● use the Look–Say–Cover–Write–Check approach to learning to spell words. Parents may need careful, explicit demonstrations of this method if they did not encounter it in their school days.
● hear their child spell for fun.
● help their child to be aware of spellings around them, for example instructions on videos or washing machines; road signs; food labels. This awareness does not mean that the child has to learn the spellings, but it helps to impress the importance of written communication as part of everyday life.

Above all, stress to parents that learning sessions should be brief and fun, and should always include plenty of praise for effort and progress. Involving parents in this way helps to develop a positive attitude in the child, which is such an important part of becoming an effective and independent speller.

How to correct spellings

Encouraging children to identify problem words and tricky parts of words for themselves begins the process of developing a 'spelling conscience', which is an important part of being an effective speller. At all times, encourage children to look up and check words they are unsure of, or words which do not 'look right'. There will be occasions when you need to correct children's spelling in the course of written work. Some useful tips for correcting children's work sensitively are:
● Concentrate on correcting misspellings of words that the child ought to know how to spell at this stage (as class teacher you are in the best position to judge what these are). This not only guarantees the best use of (your) marking time but is also less demotivating for the child.
● Don't let misspellings get in the way of praise for overall writing content.
● Try to distinguish between misspelled words that should be familiar to the child, and those which are guesses at spelling new words. Judge the latter as guesses and praise good attempts – for example, the number of 'correct' letters or a good

approximation to the sound of the word or evident use of analogy (even if it is wrong).
- Whenever possible, write the whole word correctly for the child in the margin. Do not correct parts of words in the child's writing – this only confuses the writer.

Testing and assessment

Persistent misspellings are often a problem and it is important to give specific attention to children who are not progressing. Individual error analysis, not unlike the miscue analysis developed for reading, enables teachers to look more closely at the types of errors a child is making. Repeated misspellings of particular consonants, problems with spelling prefixes or vowel digraphs can be given special attention. Although time-consuming, such analysis gives important and useful information about particular areas of spelling weakness, which can then be targeted.

A simple grid can be developed to do this:

Individual error analysis sheet

		Type of error					
Correct word	Attempted spelling	initial consonant	final consonant	consonant blend	vowel	digraph	omission
cat	kat	X					
bed	bet		X				
stop	slop			X			
run	ran				X		
feet	fet					X	
ship	sip					X	

A photocopiable version of this grid can be found on page 27.

Screening tests

When Sybil Hannovy worked at the Cambridge Institute of Education, she constructed some tests that could be given to up to 20 children at a time by one teacher with another teacher in attendance. The tests take 45–60 minutes to administer. Though designed for children younger than seven years old, the writing parts of Hannovy's tests can be adapted for use with older children who are experiencing spelling difficulties.

We expect seven-year-olds to be able to hear and discriminate all the letter sounds and names as well as to be able to write them, but this is not always the case. Older children may also have difficulty with sound–symbol relationships, and knowledge of sound–symbol correspondence is a vital element in learning both to read and spell.

The following four tests are adaptations of some of Hannovy's tests that apply to the written aspects of literacy. Extend or amend the tests further to suit the needs of particular children in your class. The first three tests highlight the child's ability to connect phonemes with letters (the auditory aspects of spelling).

In the early stages of literacy acquisition, it is essential that children are able to make connections between what they hear and what they write. Once they can hear sounds correctly and can transfer what they hear into written forms, then they are ready to progress to the visual and memory stage. Research indicates that the number of letters children can identify before they start school is the strongest predictor of subsequent reading ability.

There should be no writing or alphabets visible while the children are taking the tests. You may wish to put folded screens of card between the children to prevent copying. However, this is unnecessary if only a few children are being tested.

1. Letter sounds

Say a word to the children, and repeat the initial sound. The children write the initial letter. Walk round to observe how each child is holding their pen or pencil; look at their writing posture and letter formation. Children who cannot write the answer may leave a space. Make sure that all the letters of the alphabet are tested, but not in alphabetical order. The letters *x, q* and *y* could be merely said aloud, using their letter names. Include words with common initial digraphs and blends, repeating the initial digraph or blend (for example, ***ship, th**is, **ch**ip, **Ph**ilip, **cl**ock, **qu**ick, **sl**id, **br**ight*). The complexity of vocabulary digraphs or blends you choose will depend on the written work of your class.

Using the results

This test highlights those letters with which children are having difficulty. Many letter sounds are similar in the way they are made. For example, the letter sounds *b, g* and *d* sound similar. In linguistics, these sounds are called stops since they 'stop' the air. Other sounds that are similar are the fricatives (made by the friction or restriction of breath in a narrow opening) such as *s, z, v, f* and *th* (as in ***then*** and ***th**in*, which some children hear and pronounce as *ven* or *fin*). The short vowel sounds (as in *pat, pet, pit, pot, put*) are also formed in similar ways (the tongue is held in slightly different positions as voiced air passes through the mouth) and can cause problems for novice writers of any age. Children who have taken the test and confused letters or left spaces may:
- be unable to differentiate aurally between certain letters, or
- lack knowledge of the correspondence between sounds and the formation of their written representation.

Having identified children's specific difficulties, you are in a position to target teaching on problem letters. Help children to identify their problem letters singly and within words aurally, before transferring them to their written form. Once single-letter difficulties have been remedied, move on to blends and digraphs that are difficult for the children. Demonstrate how 'difficult' sounds, blends and digraphs are made by exaggerating their oral formation.

2. Written vocabulary

Ask the children to write all the words they can remember in five (or more) minutes. It is essential that, at the end of the test, they read all their words aloud to the teacher to check their ability to read aloud their own writing. Some children might write *came*, for example, but then say *come*.

Using the results

This test indicates the general extent of words that the child can recall and write 'easily'. Use these 'known' words to construct further dictation exercises to improve and remedy spelling difficulties. Since these words will generally be those that the child can write confidently, they should make a good balance between new and past successful learning.

The test also reveals whether a child confuses formation of certain letters. For example, having written *wat* or *bog*, the child may say *wet* and *dog* when reading the words aloud after the test. The first error indicates confusion about the pronunciation of short vowel sounds. The second error indicates the confusion of *b* and *d*, which is a common characteristic of novice readers and writers.

To remedy the first error, spend time with the child, identifying confused vowel sounds both in isolation and within words. To tackle the second, ensure that the child is in fact able to differentiate between the sounds in spoken words. Then suggest that the child says *bat and ball* to him- or herself when forming the letter *b* (as the downstroke is formed, the child says *bat*, and as the circular movement is made, the child says *ball*). Similarly, when the child hears the *d* sound in a word, he or she should say *drum and stick* to him- or herself (as the circular part is formed, he or she says *drum* and he or she says *stick* as the downstroke is formed).

3. Three phonemes

Dictate approximately 20 three-letter words to the children for them to write down (Hannovy suggested ten words for Year 1 children). The words should include as many different consonants as possible and all the vowels (for example, *rap, beg, cot, dim, fun, hop, jig, keg, lap, sat, van, win, fox, yes, zip*). The four-letter words *quit* and *very* could be included to check the *q* sound and *y* as a vowel sound. Words containing letters and sounds that seem to be causing difficulties for particular children should also be included.

Using the results

This test reveals the child's ability to hear and differentiate consonants at the beginning and end of words, and vowel sounds within words. It reveals the child's ability to spell phonically regular words – that is, their ability to blend phonemes as well as to identify them within a given word. This test can reveal whether children can hear first and last letters clearly but not the middle vowel. For example, they might write *pn* for *pin*. Use the results of the test to work with children on specific difficulties, using letters both in isolation and in three- or four-letter words spoken and written by the child. Subsequently, incorporate the words into brief sentences for the child to write and say regularly until he or she can write them fluently. Such sentences will be very obviously contrived, but in the early stages of remediation, a child's success in the learning task is of paramount importance. Success leads to increased self-confidence and motivates the child to learn more. Keep such targeted teaching sessions brief, regular and explicit, and praise effort as well as success.

4. Sentence dictation

Dictate between four and six sentences, reading each one several times, slowly. The sentences should contain words that are familiar to the children, both aurally and visually. They should include regular and irregular spellings in terms of sound–letter correspondence. The Dolch list of high-frequency words (see page 23) is a good source of such words, as are the high- and medium-frequency lists in the National Literacy Strategy *Framework for Teaching*.

Using the results

This test gives information on the general spelling strategies used by the child. These examples are taken from three children's answers to a dictation test. The dictation sentences were:

He went in the house and saw a man.
The man was doing some magic tricks.

Child A wrote:

He went in the huose and saw a man.
The man was doing some magick tricks.

Child A shows only two errors. The first error, *huose*, contains all the correct letters, indicating visual recall of the word, but with confused recall of the *ou* sequence. The second error, *magick*, may be influenced by the spelling of the next word, *trick*. Once the child has identified and underlined the errors, look at other words in the *ou* family (for example, ***out, our, loud, mouse***), and discuss the use of *c* and *ck* as word endings. Construct a sentence for the child to learn and be tested on over the following few days (for example, *I went **out** of **our** **h**ouse with the magi**c** man*). If reversals of *ou* persist, compose a mnemonic for the *ou* sequence (for example, ***Oh you** are in my h**ou**se*).

Child B wrote:

He wet in the hows and saw a man.
The man woss dowing sum majik trix.

Child B shows that most (if not all) letter sounds are known, as many of the words are written according to their sound. Child B is still at what may be termed the 'invented' spelling stage. This child has minimal knowledge of high-frequency words with irregular sound–letter correspondence (for example, *he, saw, the*).

Show Child B explicitly how to look at problem words carefully and to identify the tricky parts for him- or herself. Use the child's errors to do this. For example, when looking at the word *doing* (which the child spelled *dowing*), praise him or her for having nearly all the correct letters, before asking him or her to spot the incorrect letter. Ask the child to use Look–Say–Cover–Write–Check to learn the words *do, doing, go, going*. To remedy *woss* for *was*, encourage the child to locate the word *as* within *was*.

Construct a sentence for the child to learn and be tested on over the following few days (for example, *He **was** not **do**ing his jobs, he was **go**ing in the hut*). Note that the 'new' words in the sentence are phonically regular and so should not cause difficulties for the child.

Adjust the learning load to suit different children's levels of difficulty and attention span.

> **Child C** wrote:
> *He we in the os a se a ma.*
> *The ma wos dwig mha tx.*

Child C's attempts at written communication have broken down completely. This child knows how to spell *he*, *in* and *the*, but leaves many words unfinished. Initial letters of words are generally correct; *os* for *house* indicates that the *h* has not been heard, or that the child is hearing the *o* and *s* sound more dominantly. This child's spelling strategies are characteristic of someone at the very earliest stage of learning to write and who has learned a few high-frequency words by heart. Identifying separate letters in words and blending letters will help this child.

Helping children with spelling difficulties

Regular reading and writing activities will help most children to become confident and efficient spellers. However, some children will find that learning to spell presents difficulties, and there are specific but varying causes for this. One cause is dyslexia whereby something goes wrong with a person's perception of words and letters. This often affects the ability to read and write. However, if teaching is tailored to individual needs, specific difficulties may be overcome. It is important, therefore, to try to find out the individual causes of these difficulties before attempts are made to remedy them.

Remediation may include teaching/revising one or more of the following:
- sound–symbol correspondence of the alphabet, including names of letters
- common and regular letter strings which may include the use of plastic letters
- awareness of irregular but high-frequency words in which the visual aspects of the words are studied
- clear articulation of words to be studied and clear articulation of the letters of the words (in sequence)
- multi-sensory approaches to the Look–Say–Cover–Write–Check method
- use of computers, word-processors, coloured pens and so on to aid motivation in learning
- use of mnemonics to aid learning
- regular use of wordbanks once spelling is improving
- very brief, but regular, informal tests on one or two sentences which contain the words learned – the aim is to ensure the child's success.

Using plastic letters to improve literacy
A useful tool for helping children with spelling difficulties is the use of plastic letters in instruction. Some research shows that less able readers (and spellers) may be unsuccessful in the aural medium since it seems too abstract. Working with the concrete and tangible, such as plastic letters, can help these children. When word building with plastic letters, keep the focus letters static while moving other letters

around them. (For example, the blend *an* is kept static while *c, m, p, h* and *d, s* and *d* are placed in front and behind to make the words *an, can, man, pan, hand, sand*). Increase the complexity and difficulty of letter strings as the child progresses.

Look–Say–Cover–Write–Check

Expand the method into the following multi-sensory approach for children with difficulties. Children should:

1. **Look** carefully at the word.
2. **Say** the word and then its letters (names) in sequence.
3. **Cover** the word up.
4. **'Write'** the word, saying the whole word first, then the letter names:
   - in the air with eyes closed, or
   - on an (imaginary) desk, or
   - in wet sand.
   If all appears to be correct, then say the word and its letters to the teacher. Write the word on paper or in a wordbank (saying the word and letter names while doing so).
5. **Check** the word. If it is correct, write a tick over each correct letter, adding an extra tick if all the letters are in the correct order*.

*This way, the child feels more involved in his or her learning and progress than if the teacher takes the child's work and applies ticks (or crosses). For example, *house* would receive six ticks (one for each correct letter, and one for the correct sequence); *huose* would receive five ticks; and *hows* four ticks (one for each correct letter and one because they are in the correct order).

These procedures may seem time-consuming, but they usually apply only to a few children with severe spelling difficulties.

Motivating children with spelling difficulties

Using ICT can help to motivate children who find spelling difficult, particularly older children who are more likely to be negative in their attitude towards remedial teaching than younger ones. Word-processing, for example, can be helpful in giving higher status to the writing process – the work produced is clear and professional, and inputting words on-screen reinforces understanding of the left-to-right sequence of writing. Increasingly, even very young children are able to find their way round technological equipment, sometimes more easily than adults.

Encourage children to use computer spellcheckers. They will not impede the process of learning to spell and can be a useful aid, if children know about the pitfalls of using them. Make sure they understand that spellcheckers do not eliminate errors entirely as they cannot recognise grammatical relationships in sentences. It is important that children know when to 'overrule' the spellchecker.

Once confidence in spelling has been restored, and progress made and maintained, children should balance traditional methods of writing with using the computer. The use of coloured pens, pencils and paper can also stimulate children's motivation.

Bibliography

Bryant, PE & Bradley, L (1985) *Rhyme and Reason in Reading and Spelling,* University of Michigan Press.

DfEE/QCA (1999) *The National Curriculum: Handbook for Primary Teachers in England.*

Department of Education Northern Ireland (1996) *The Northern Ireland Curriculum Key Stages 1 and 2.*

Ehri, LC (1991) 'Learning to read and spell words' in L Rieben and C Perfetti (eds) *Learning to Read: Basic Research and its Implications,* Lawrence Erlbaum Associates.

Goswami, U & Bryant, PE (1990) *Phonological Skills and Learning to Read,* Lawrence Erlbaum Associates.

Hannovy, S (1991) 'Middle infant screening test: a safety net for teachers' in *Reading,* 25, no. 3, 10–15, Blackwell for UKRA.

Morris, JM (1984) 'Phonics 44 for initial literacy in English' in *Reading,* 18, no. 1, Blackwell for UKRA.

Mudd, NR (1994) *Effective Spelling: A practical guide for teachers,* Hodder & Stoughton in association with UKRA.

Peters, ML (1985) *Spelling: Caught or Taught? (A New Look),* Routledge.

The Scottish Office Education Department (1991) *National Guidelines English Language 5–14.*

Temple, C, Nathan, R, Burris, N & Temple, F (1993 3rd edition) *The Beginnings of Writing,* Allyn and Bacon Inc.

Todd, J (1982) *Learning to Spell: A Book of Resources for Teachers,* Simon & Schuster.

Teaching content and skills grid

- Focuses on rhyme, with children's attention being drawn to what they see as well as what they hear.
- Reminds children of the modification of vowels which frequently but not always occurs when words end in *e*. (This is referred to as *magic e*.)
- Requires children to play an active role in identifying recurring letter patterns and tricky parts in words by underlining them.
- Explains use of syllabification in spelling and saying longer words.
- Makes continued reference to the use of personal wordbanks and the Look–Say–Cover–Write–Check method of learning spellings.
- Introduces children to using dictionaries and arranging words in alphabetical order, some of which begin with the same letter.
- Encourages children to proof-read their own and others' writing.
- Introduces children to some words of French origin.

The grid on the facing page matches teaching content to pages.

List of the 44 phonemes in English

20 vowel sounds

Short vowel sounds

apple
egg
ink
orange
umbrella
p**o**tato (this has an indistinct
vowel sound or *schwa*)

Long vowel sounds

ape	p**ai**n	s**ay**
eve	p**ee**l	s**ea**l
ice	l**ie**	h**igh**
m**o**de	s**oa**k	t**oe**
fl**u**te	p**oo**l	

Other vowel sounds

b**a**ll	w**a**lk	s**aw**
st**ar**		
b**ir**d	h**er**mit	
h**oo**k		
m**ou**th	cl**ow**n	
c**oi**l	b**oy**	
sq**uare**	ch**air**	
ear	d**eer**	h**ere**
g**our**d	p**oor**	

24 consonant sounds

bat
cat (**k**it)
din
fish
go
have
jump
let
man
net
pat
run
set
tap
violin
want
yet
zoo (hou**s**es)
shop
chin
the
thing
si**ng**
televi**si**on

Some other consonant patterns

double consonants: *ff, ck*
clusters (initial): *sk, sp, st, cl, cr, scr, str*
clusters (end): *sk, sp, st, ps, nds, nks*
silent letters: *knit, thumb*

NB *q* and *x* are redundant as 'basic' phonemes.

Dolch list

These 100 words make up, on average, one half of all reading.

a	and	he
I	in	is
it	of	that
the	to	was
all	as	at
be	but	are
for	had	have
his	him	not
on	one	said
so	they	we
with	you	about
an	back	been
before	big	by
call	came	can
come	could	did
do	down	first
from	get	go
has	her	here
if	into	just
like	little	look
made	make	more
me	much	must
my	no	new
now	off	old
only	or	our
other	out	over
right	see	she
some	their	them
then	there	this
two	up	want
well	went	were
what	when	where
which	will	who
your		

The 100 next most used words.

after	again	always
am	another	any
away	ask	bad
because	best	bird
black	blue	boy
bring	day	dog
don't	eat	every
far	fast	father
fell	find	five
fly	four	found
gave	girl	give
going	good	got
green	hand	have
head	help	home
house	how	jump
keep	know	last
left	let	live
long	man	many
may	men	mother
Mr	never	next
once	open	own
play	put	ran
read	red	room
round	run	sat
saw	say	school
should	sing	sit
soon	stop	take
tell	than	these
thing	think	three
time	too	tree
under	us	very
walk	white	why
wish	work	would
year		

Am I a good speller?

	often	sometimes	never
I know that correct spelling is important.			
I always stop to check a spelling if I am unsure			
• by checking in my wordbank			
• by checking in a dictionary.			
I always proof-read by looking for spelling mistakes.			
I take care with my handwriting.			
I notice letter patterns like **th** and **ough**.			
I notice suffixes like **-less**.			
I notice prefixes like **dis-**.			
I learn new spellings using Look–Say–Cover–Write–Check.			
I make up mnemonics to help me remember spellings.			
My tricky words are			

Name _____   Date _____

Indicators for novice spellers

Spelling confidence:	often	sometimes	never
spells known words automatically			
interested in new words			
tackles spellings of new words with intelligent guesses			
Spelling conscience:			
proof-reads own writing			
checks words unsure of			
● using the wordbank			
● using a dictionary			
Spelling skills:			
aware of visual patterns			
recognises many common words			
is able to spell many common words			
uses words with irregular spellings			
attempts to spell new words by analogy			
uses syllabification to learn longer words			
uses mnemonics			
understands compound words			
uses common prefixes and suffixes			
recognises roots of words			
aware that there are different ways of spelling a sound			

Name   Date

Record of progress

Units		Date completed
1	What did you do on your holiday?	
2	A visit to the zoo	
3	Changing meanings	
4	Syllable splits	
5	Unusual and tricky	
6	Rhymes and riddles (1)	
7	Rhymes and riddles (2)	
8	Scissors	
9	That's funny	
10	Attention!	
11	Ferry cross the Mersey	
12	Great days out	
13	Double trouble	
14	Visiting the shops	
15	Brrr! It's freezing!	
16	What's cooking?	
17	Singular or plural?	
18	A birthday treat	
19	Foggy and frosty	
20	Cry, cried and crying	
21	Sports mad	
22	Football facts	
23	The sporting life	
24	It, its or it's?	
24	There, there...	
16	Using a dictionary	
27	Smelly socks	
28	Knights in armour	
29	Remember, remember!	
30	Sort of brown	

Name   Date

Individual error analysis sheet

Correct word	Attempted spelling	Type of error					
		initial consonant	final consonant	consonant blend	vowel	digraph	omission

Name

Objectives: Spell words with the *a* sound as in *pain*. Spell *quite* and *quiet*.

Unit **1**

What did you do on your holiday?

1. Read about what these people did on their holiday. With a partner, take it in turns to read what each child says.

David:	I went to Spain and it rained. Each day, I became quite wet.
Jennifer:	I went to the beach by train. The sea was quite rough.
Tom:	I helped Dad dig drains and paint the fence.
Adam:	I helped Mum put down snail bait. Snails love rainy weather.
Sam:	I remained at home waiting for mail. I'm afraid it was a very quiet holiday!
Jill:	I rode my trail bike until I sprained my ankle. I had to rest for quite a long time.
Mike:	I helped Grandpa catch worms for bait. We worked very quietly.

2. Look carefully at the spellings in the passage, especially **ai** words and **quite/quiet**.

If you mix up **quite/quiet** when you are writing, this sentence may help you remember when to use **quite**:

I had quite a big bite.   (Qu**ite** and b**ite** end in **ite**.)

3. Put the sentence into your wordbank next to **quite**.

4. Now write out the whole passage, one sentence at a time, in your workbook. Check! Underline the **a** as in p**ai**n words.

5. Write about what you did on holiday on a rainy day in your workbook. After you have finished, read your work *slowly* to yourself so that you can check it.

28 Scholastic Literacy Skills
Spelling Ages 8–9

Photocopiable ■ SCHOLASTIC Continued on P29

Name

Continued from P28

6. Look at these two lists of words. Join the words that rhyme. One has been done for you.

nail	raise
maid	aim
praise	main
claim	tail
pain	afraid

7. Say these verses aloud, using the words in the box to finish the rhymes.

> paint   aid   tail   complain

My little cat gave out a wail

Because the door had caught his t_____.

You catch the bus, you catch the train

I've never heard you once c_____.

My head is spinning, I feel quite faint

It must be using that awful p_____.

Don't be worried, don't be afraid

The emergency services will come to your a_____.

8. When you think you know the four verses, write them down in your workbook.

9. After looking carefully at spellings which may be tricky for you, write them in your wordbank. Check!

A visit to the zoo

1. Read the story.

> Mum and I went to the zoo in the school holidays. My brother came too. We saw lions, tigers, elephants, camels, seals and orang-utans. I liked the orang-utans best. They looked like my brother and me. My mum said she liked the seals but my brother preferred the elephants.
>
> We took our lunch to the zoo and ate it at a picnic table. My brother and I ate sandwiches and crisps. My mum had packed fruit too. She gave some to my brother and me.

 In this story **too** means 'as well' or 'also'.

2. Look carefully at any spellings which may be tricky for you. Look, say, cover and write each word in your wordbank, then check.

3. When you think you know the spellings, write the story in your workbook.

4. Read these sentences, filling in the gaps with **too** or **to**.

He went t_____ Blackpool for his holidays.

My friend has a telephone. I have one t_____.

She came t_____ my house in July and her brother came t_____.

We went t_____ the beach and swam all day.

Our dog swam t_____.

Continued from P30   Unit **2**

5. Write the sentences in your workbook.

6. Read these sentences aloud.

I like to go with Mum to the zoo.

Pete and I walked home.

Dad took me to the park.

Uncle Ted gave me an ice cream.

  Is it **I** or **me?**

When **you** are doing the verb – for example, **I like** or **I walked**, then it is always **I**.

7. Now read these sentences aloud, putting **I** or **me** in the spaces.

That girl gave _____ a funny look.

My brother and _____ ate ice cream.

I hope Dad comes to the museum with _____.

John, Ann and _____ walked home.

8. Now write all the sentences again here.

_____

_____

_____

_____

Objective: Change meanings of words with the prefix *non*.

Unit **3**

Changing meanings

1. Say these words.

stop	non-stop
payment	non-payment
slip	non-slip
member	non-member

2. Write down what you think **non** means.

_____

3. Now write the words on the left in your wordbank, and then the **non** words by their side (as above).

Non comes from Latin and means 'not'.

Non is often joined to words by a hyphen (-), for example **non-stop**. Sometimes there is no hyphen, for example **nonsense**.

4. Change the meanings of these words by adding non.

human _____   smoking _____

fiction _____   stop _____

stick_____   sense _____

5. Choose three **non** words and write a sentence for each one in your workbook. There is one here to start you off.

For example: Our train goes **non-stop** to Inverness.

Photocopiable ◣ SCHOLASTIC Continued on P33

Objectives: Change meanings of words with the prefix *non*. Change meanings by adding the suffixes *less* and *ful*.

Continued from P32

Unit **3**

> **less** means 'without'
>
> **ful** means 'full of'

6. Read these words aloud.

faith	friend	hat	cheer
hope	end	shame	speech

7. Now write the words in your wordbank, adding the suffix **less** to each one. For example, **faith – faithless**. What happens to the meaning of each word?

8. Read these sentences aloud, then write them down in your workbook.

He was quite friendless and this made him sad.

The morning seemed endless.

She was speechless when she read the letter about her non-payment of a bill.

John is hopeful that his team will win – his mother is hopeful too.

9. Write out the **less**, **full** and **non** words. Next to each word, write what it means. Continue on the back of this sheet. Here is one to start you off.

Friendless means without friends.

_____

_____

_____

Syllable splits

1. Say these words aloud. Write them side by side in your wordbank.

gate	gateway	be	being
sea	seaside	free	freedom
paint	painted	clean	cleaning

Gate has one syllable. **Gateway** has two syllables, **gate way**.

Syllables can help you to spell: you spell the words in parts; you hear the parts as you say the words.

2. Write the two syllables in each of these words. The first one has been done for you.

painter _pain ter_____

doing _____

freeing _____

cleanest _____

3. Here are some more words. If they have one syllable, put a circle around the whole word. If they have more than one syllable, underline the syllables, for example: **visitor** has three syllables, **vis it or**.

beach	camping	skiing	visitor	non-stop
plane	sailor	ticket	sunshine	train

4. Write any new words in your wordbank. Remember to Look–Say–Cover–Write–Check! Look very carefully at the two **ii**s in sk**ii**ng.

Name

Objectives: Split words into syllables.
Add *suffixes* to words.

Continued from P34

Unit 4

5. Read these sentences aloud, then write them down in your workbook.

The sailor went non-stop round the world.

We had the cleanest caravan.

The skier was doing what he liked best.

Who was the visitor to our campsite?

6. Choose from the **suffixes** in the box to make these one-syllable words into two-syllable words.

> ing   er   less   ful

train_____   fail_____   brain_____

pain_____   rain_____

7. Say these words slowly, listening for each syllable. Look at the whole words and then parts of them. Then split them into syllables. The first one has been done for you.

caravan   <u>car a van</u>

deckchair   _____

packing   _____

rocket   _____

unlucky   _____

seaside   _____

beating   _____

Unusual and tricky

When we change verbs to the past tense, we often add **ed** to the **root** (the main part of the verb).

present tense	**past tense**
I sail	I sail**ed**
You walk	You walk**ed**

1. However, the above rule is not always what happens. Read these unusual past tenses, say them aloud, then match each one with its present tense from the box.

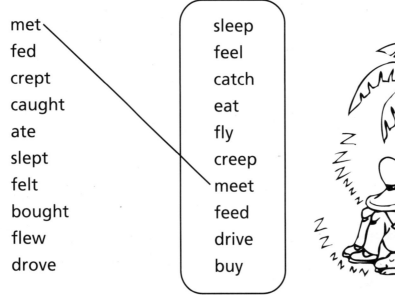

met
fed
crept
caught
ate
slept
felt
bought
flew
drove

sleep
feel
catch
eat
fly
creep
meet
feed
drive
buy

2. Now write each pair of words in your wordbank.

3. Write four sentences of your own using some of the unusual past tenses. Here is one to start you off.

Mum drove us to the airport.

_____

_____

_____

_____

Continued from P36

4. Say these words carefully: **our   are   or**

Can you hear the difference between them? If you sometimes get these words mixed up, these sentences may help you remember which is which.

our	He was in **ou**r ho**u**se.
are	They **ar**e in the c**ar**.
or	Come f**or** me, **or** I will go!

5. Say them aloud, making sure you pronounce **our**, **are** and **or** correctly.

6. Now write the words **our**, **are** and **or** in your wordbank. Write the sentence for each word to help you remember how to spell it.

7. Read these tricky words and underline the tricky parts. Then write the words down in your workbook.

pretty	friend	when	mother	toilet
what	busy	walked	talked	chalk

8. Now read these sentences aloud (to help you learn tricky spellings).

B**e**tty is pr**e**tty.

I saw my **fri**end on **Fri**day.

The **other** lady was his m**other**.

When I saw the **hen**, I ran away.

She poured **oil** in the t**oil**et and sp**oil**ed it!

What a silly **hat**!

The **bus** is **bus**y.

Name _____

Look at these words.

Say them aloud.

Cover each set of words.

Write them in your workbook.

Check to see if you are right.

train	Spain	paint
Be quiet!	remain	
quite a bit	afraid	praise
complain	raise	
prefer	fruit	Mum and I talked.
preferred	She came too.	
walk	ice cream	visitor
holidays	walked	
sense	nonsense	stick
faithless	non-stick	
cheerful	seaside	doing
cleanest	freedom	

When you have written each set of words, CHECK them to see if they are right. If they are right, put a tick. If any are wrong, cross them out. Look carefully at the correct word(s) again, note where you went wrong and write them again in your wordbank.

There are 36 words (not counting **a**, **I** and **and**). How many did you get right first time?

Name

Continued from P38

1. She asked me and my brother to come home.

2. If you fed the plants every day, then I could feed them too.

3. Our caravan is in a field near our house.

4. She shouted, "You might have told me that I had slept until twelve!"

5. The visitor crept over to the deckchair.

6. He ate ice cream, crisps and sweets too.

7. Have you caught any fish here?

8. I saw my friend on Friday – or was it Saturday?

9. Al walked and talked all day last Wednesday.

10. What have you bought him for his birthday?

Look at these sentences.

Say them aloud.

Cover each sentence.

Write them in your workbook.

Check to see if you are right.

Do the same with these sentences. You can WRITE, then CHECK after each sentence.

How many sentences were correct?

Enter any words that were not correct into your wordbank under the correct letter. Do this even if the word is there already.

Name

Objectives: Spell words with the *i* sound as in *by* and *goodbye*. Spell *y*, *ye* and *eye* words.

Unit 6

Rhymes and riddles (1)

1. Read this funny playground rhyme, filling in the missing words. Underline the words which have the **i** as in **by** sound.

> A Pesky Little _____
>
> A pesky little _____
> said, "Catch me, go on, tr_____.
> I'm too quick for you, small fr_____!"
>   Smack
> "Good_____, fl_____!"
> *Gordon Winch*

The word goodbye comes from '**God b**e with **y**ou!'

2. Say and listen to the **i** as in **by** sound in these words.

> by   cry   dry   fly

3. Finish these words with the letter which spells the **i** sounds. Write them in your wordbank.

fr_____   m_____   tr_____   wh_____

Dye and **rye** have the **i** sound too.

5. Complete these sentences by filling in the missing words.

The d_____ in my shirt is dark red.

You can use r_____ flour to make bread.

 Continued on P41

Name

Objectives: Spell words with the *i* sound as in *by* and *goodbye*. Spell *y*, *ye* and *eye* words.

Continued from P40

Unit 6

6. Now make up and write in your workbook five sentences or a funny poem using some of the **i** sound words on the last page.

7. Solve this riddle. Fill in the missing letters.

Why is the letter j like your nose?

Answer: Because it is next to **i** (e_____).

8. Solve these riddles too by filling in the missing letters.

Why did the dog tr_____ to bite his tail?

Answer: He was tr_____ing to make ends meet.

What is the best day to cook fish?

Answer: F_____day.

FISH DISHES

9. Read these sentences aloud, filling in the spaces with the **i** sound. Then complete the sentences, using **y**, **ye** or **eye**.

He will always tr_____ to trick you. He is very sl_____.

"Clean this room," said mum. "It's like a pig st_____."

"Wh_____ are you cr_____ing?" asked the teacher.

"I have something in m_____ e_____ ," I yelled.

10. Now write the sentences in your workbook. Then swap with a partner and check spellings and your punctuation.

Name _____

Objective: Spell words with the *i* sound as in *pie*.

Unit 7

Rhymes and riddles (2)

 Some **i** sounds are spelt with **ie**.

1. Finish this funny rhyme with **ie** spellings.

Simple Simon met a p_____ man

Going to the fair.

Said Simple Simon to the man,

"What have you got there?"

"P_____ s, stupid!"

2. Make **i** as in p**ie** words with these consonants and write them in your wordbank.

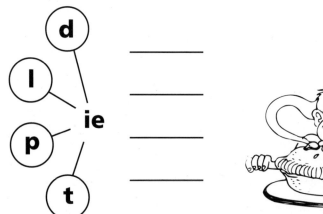

d

l   ie

p

t

_____
_____
_____
_____

3. Finish these sentences using the words in the box.

> die   lie   tie

He is too young to _____.

_____ down on the bed.

I cannot tell a _____. I tipped sauce on your _____.

Objective: Spell words with the *i* as in *pie* sound.

Continued from P42

4. Finish these riddles, filling in the gaps with **ie** words.

What kind of bow is impossible to t_____?

Answer: A rainbow.

What is the left side of an apple p_____?

Answer: The side no one has eaten.

Watch out for these words. They sound the same but have different spellings.

> **dye** – colour   **die** – to stop living

Words that sound the same are called **homophones** (same sounds).

5. Circle the correct word to finish these sentences.

"I am too young to (dye die)," said the fly.

I will (die dye) my pullover green.

I laughed so much I thought I would (die dye).

6. Use the clues to complete this crossword with **i** as in p**ie** words.

Down
1. A grain.
2. To stop living.

Across
2. A colour in your clothes.
3. A hot meat-____ .

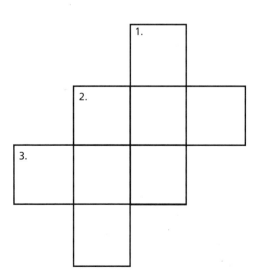

Name

Scissors

1. Read this funny poem aloud.

Scissors

Nobody leave the room.
Everyone listen to me.
We had ten pairs of scissors
At half-past two,
And now there's only three.

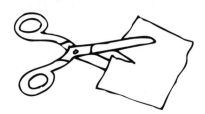

Seven pairs of scissors
Disappeared from sight.
Not one of you leaves
Till we find them
We can stop here all night!

Scissors don't lose themselves,
Melt away or explode.
Scissors have not got
Legs of their own
To go running off up the road.

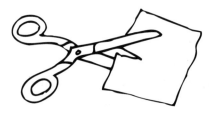

We really need those scissors,
That's what makes me mad.
If it was seven pairs
Of children we'd lost,
It wouldn't be so bad.

I don't want to hear excuses.
Don't anyone speak.
Just ransack this room
Till we find them,
Or we'll stop here... all week!

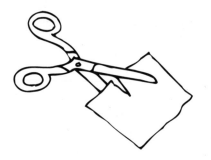

Allan Ahlberg

2. Write out the two verses you like best in your workbook. Take care with the tricky word **scissors**.

 Continued on P45

Name

Objectives: Spell words with *silent c* as in *scissors*. Spell words with the vowel *o* and *magic e*.

Continued from P44   Unit **8**

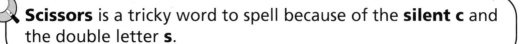 **Scissors** is a tricky word to spell because of the **silent c** and the double letter **s**.

3. Look at these words with **silent c**. Look at them carefully and read them aloud. Now cover and write them in your workbook.

| scent | science | scene | scythe |
| scented | scientist | scenery | scissors |

4. Write three sentences in your workbook, using **sc** words.

5. Write these **ode** and **one** words. Write them in your wordbank.

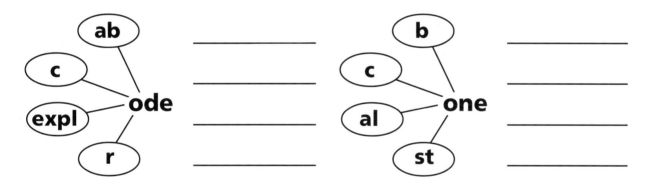

6. Use a dictionary to check the meaning of **abode**. Write the meaning next to the word in your wordbank.

 When we add **e** to words, it often (but not always) gives the vowel its letter name. For example: **ton + e = tone**.

The short vowel **o** sound in **ton** changes to the long vowel **o** sound in **tone**. We call this **e magic e**.

7. Complete these **ode** and **one** words.

She r_____ her bicycle.

He was al_____ when the fireworks began to expl_____ .

Name

That's funny

1. Read this poem aloud.

Benjamin Drew

Said the teacher to Benjamin Drew,
"You never say 'youse' you say 'you'.
It's a pain and an ache
To hear that mistake.
Once more and you're into the stew."

Gordon Winch

Do not be like Benjamin Drew. Make sure you know how to use and spell **you**, **your**, **you're** and **yours**.

We use **your** and **yours** to show that something belongs to you.

For example:

This is **your** book.   This book is **yours**.

You're is short for **you are**. We put an apostrophe to show where the letter **a** has been left out.

2. Complete these sentences, filling in the spaces using **you**, **your**, **you're** or **yours**.

_____ must not be like Benjamin Drew.

_____ spelling must be correct.

I think that mine is correct. Let me see _____ .

Please phone me when _____ ready to go.

 Continued on P47

Objective: Spell *you, your, you're* and *yours.*

Continued from ▸ P46

Unit **9**

3. Do you know what a **tall story** is? Read this story and perhaps you will be able to guess. **You**, **your**, **you're** or **yours** is left out of each space. Add the correct word as you read.

The three farmers

There were three farmers, talking about the size of their

animals. "_____ have never seen bigger cows than

mine," said the first farmer. "They are so big _____

need a ladder to milk them. They are much bigger than any

animals of _____ ."

"_____ think _____ cows are big," said the

second farmer. "Our sheep are so large that when we shear

them, one fleece is enough to make jumpers for five

football teams."

"Pretty big livestock," said the third farmer. "But

_____ are not big enough to beat ours. Do you see

that jumbo jet flying over my farm? It's not a jumbo jet; it's

one of our ducks."

"_____ joking!" said the first and second farmers.

4. Do you know what **livestock** means? If you split the word into syllables **live stock** you may be able to guess. Now use a dictionary to check if you are right!

5. In your workbook, write what you think a tall story is. Then write the complete story.

Objective: Spell *tion* words.

Attention!

Remember that the letters **tion** sound like **shun**.

1. Say these **tion** words aloud. They have been split into syllables. If you say each syllable, it may help you to spell them.

station	(**sta tion**)	mention	(**men tion**)
relation	(**re la tion**)	prevention	(**pre ven tion**)
lotion	(**lo tion**)	national	(**na tion al**)

2. Now cover the words and write them in your wordbank.

3. Read these sentences aloud, filling in the spaces with the correct **tion** word. Then write the word in the spaces.

Go to the s_____ at once if you want to catch your train.

Is he your r_____? Yes, he's my dad!

Firemen have to learn about fire p_____ as well as how to put out fires.

Do not go out in the strong sunlight without using suntan

l_____.

Don't m_____ that I broke the window.

4. Try to make sense of this silly poem. You will have to think carefully about what it says.

> YYUR
> YYUB
> ICUR
> YY for me!

 Continued on P49

5. Write what you think the poem says here. Check your answer at the bottom of the page.

_____

_____

_____

We have seen that **too** means 'as well'. For example: You can come **too**.

Too also means 'more than enough', as in the silly poem you have written.

6. Read these examples of **too** meaning 'more than enough'.

too clever	too slow
too late	too thin
too much	

7. Write four sentences here using **too** meaning 'more than enough'. Then write four sentences in your workbook using **too** meaning 'as well'.

_____

_____

_____

_____

Answer: *Too wise you are*
Too wise you be
I see you are
Too wise for me!

Name _____

Look at these words.

Say them aloud.

Cover each set of words.

Write them in your workbook.

Check to see if you are right.

by	dry	fly
cry	try/trying	
dye	cry/crying	pies
eye	why	
die	scissors	scene
goodbye	scent	
code	explode	bone
rode	tone	
alone	You're being silly.	station
phone	That's your home.	
mention	You're too quiet!	national
prevention	You're too late!	

When you have written each set of words, CHECK them to see if they are right. If they are right, put a tick. If any are wrong, cross them out. Look carefully at the correct word(s) again, note where you went wrong and write them again in your wordbank.

There are 40 words. How many did you get right first time?

Name

Continued from P50

1. The farmers think you're joking about your ducks.

2. I spy with my little eye something beginning with **b**.

3. He is too sleepy to get undressed for bed.

4. I cannot tell a lie. I lost the pie.

5. Each child had two pairs of scissors.

6. I want you to phone your sister on Wednesday.

7. On bonfire night, the fireworks exploded non-stop.

8. "Is this suntan lotion yours?" she asked.

9. Were you going to the station when you met the visitor?

Look at these sentences.

Say them aloud.

Cover each sentence.

Write them in your workbook.

Check to see if you are right.

Do the same with these sentences. (Don't forget to look at the punctuation!) You can WRITE, then CHECK after each sentence.

How many sentences were correct?

Enter any words that were not correct into your wordbank under the correct letter. Do this even if the word is there already.

Name

Ferry cross the Mersey

1. Perhaps you know this song. Read it aloud. (The Mersey is a river in Liverpool.)

Ferry cross the Mersey

Life goes on day after day,
Hearts torn in every way.
So ferry cross the Mersey
'cos this land's the place I love
and here I'll stay.

People they rush everywhere,
Each with their own secret care.
So ferry cross the Mersey
and always take me there
the place I'll stay.

Gerry Marsden

 'cos is short for **because**.

2. Underline any words in the song which end with the **i** sound as in merr**y**.

 Most words ending with the **i** sound end in **y**.

For example: only   baby

But some words ending with the **i** sound end in **ey**.

For example: monkey   key

Many surnames and place names which end in the **i** sound are spelled **ey**.

For example: Bill Bailey   Burnley

Objective: Spell words with the *i* sound as in *merry*.

Continued from P52

3. Decide whether these words end in **y** or **ey**, then write down the correct ending.

cherr_____   ver_____

mon_____   marr_____

carr_____   hon_____

penn_____   John Lawl_____

Does anyone in your class have a surname ending in **ey**?

4. Write the words that fit these clues. When you have checked that they are correct, write them in your wordbank.

to move quickly   h_____

a place where we get stone or rock   qu_____

to wed   m_____

a coin   p_____

5. Make words that end in **y** where the **y** has the sound **i** as in cher**ry**. Write them around the square as shown here. One has been done for you.

sunny

sun	Tim	fer
cher	y	fur
pen	run	tum

Name

Great days out

1. Read these sentences aloud. Underline the word **he** each time you read it. Write the sentences out in your workbook.

> Tommy visited the museum.
> He went there with his family.
> He liked looking at the skeletons of dinosaurs,
> but he didn't like waiting to get a drink.

 Tommy is a **naming word** or **noun**. The word **he** is called a **pronoun** because it is used instead of the noun **Tommy**.

2. Read these sentences aloud, underlining the word **him** each time you hear it. Then write the sentences in your workbook.

I saw Tommy going to the museum.

His family went with him.

Looking at the dinosaurs made him happy.

Waiting for a drink made him angry.

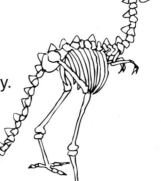

 Him is also a pronoun. It is used instead of the noun **Tommy**.

3. Here are some more pronouns. Read them aloud.

I	you	her	it	
me	she	us	they	them

4. Write down the pronouns in your workbook. Then write five sentences using some of them.

Name

Continued from P54

5. Read these words aloud, then Look–Say–Cover–Write them in your workbook. Remember to check each word.

> action   section   portion   provision
>
> vision   television   permission

 Remember that **tion** and **sion** both sound like **shun**.

6. Check the meanings of any words you do not know in a dictionary.

7. Read this story aloud.

> ## Johnny visits the theme park
>
> Johnny was glad that there was provision for his wheelchair in the theme park. His parents bought him an Action Man and he was given permission to go in the swimming pool. He was delighted! However, he was not able to see all of the park because one section was closed.
>
> When he arrived back home he was too tired to watch his favourite television programme. But that didn't matter, because he had had a super day!

8. Underline all the **sion** or **tion** words. Circle all the **possessive** pronouns.

> **His** is another pronoun. It is a **possessive** pronoun because we use it when something belongs to him.

9. Can you think of some more possessive pronouns? Write them in your workbook. Here are two to get you started.

our/ours (something belonging to us)

their/theirs (something belonging to them)

Name

Double trouble

> When the last three letters of a word end in a consonant–vowel–consonant (CVC), we *double* the final consonant when adding a suffix.

1. Look at these words. Read them aloud, then write them in your wordbank.

pat	patted	patting
fan	fanned	fanning
drip	dripped	dripping
pin	pinned	pinning
hop	hopped	hopping
hug	hugged	hugging

2. Add **ed** to these words.

wag_____ dim_____ drum_____ hum_____ rig_____

3. Add **ing** to these words.

sit_____ zap_____ wet_____ nod_____ chug_____

4. Look at these words. Add **er** then **est** to each one. Write all the words. The first one has been done for you.

fat   *fatter*   *fattest*

wet

fit

hot

Name

Objective: Know when to double consonants.

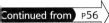

5. In your workbook, write four sentences using some of the words you have made.

> When we add the suffix **y** to words which end in CVC, we also double the last consonant.

6. Read these pairs of words aloud.

dad	daddy	run	runny
bad	baddy	pup	puppy

7. Make as many words as you can by adding **ed**, **ing**, **er**, **est** or **y** to these words. Make sure that the word has meaning.

tan _____

span _____

fun _____

dip _____

wet _____

bat _____

8. Read this story aloud. Underline all the CVC words which end in a suffix.

At the swimming pool

Tuesday was hotter than Wednesday and we went to the swimming pool. My mother was fanning herself to keep cool. My friend and I were keeping cool by sitting in the pool. When we came out we were dripping wet. It was no longer sunny!

Visiting the shops

1. Read this poem aloud and underline all the **ought** words.

> ## Visiting the shops
>
> My mum bought me new school clothes,
> They cost a lot I thought.
> My mum said they would cost much less
> Without the final nought!
>
> *Gordon Winch*

2. These **ough** words end in **t**, but the **gh** is not sounded. Say, then write these **ought** words.

b
f
ought
n
th

_____

_____

_____

_____

3. These **ough** words rhyme with **uff**. Say, then write the **ough** words.

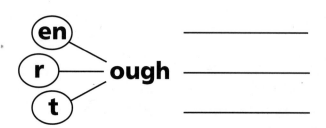

en
r — **ough**
t

_____

_____

_____

Name

Objectives: Spell *ough* and *ought* words.
Spell *through* and *though*.

 Continued from P58

Unit 14

4. These **ough** words look almost the same. One has an extra letter. What is it? Circle the extra letter.

through (sounds like **threw**)

though (rhymes with **snow**)

5. Add the words to your wordbank. Can you think of a way to remember how to spell **through**? Make sure you sound the **r** in **through** each time you say it. It may help you to remember the **r**.

6. Circle the correct word to finish these sentences.

She looked (through, though) the window.

I ate the cake (though, through) I was full.

We decided to visit our friends (though, through) it was raining.

The football flew (though, through) the air towards the goal.

The visitor looked (though, through) the letter box.

7. Read this story aloud, filling in the gaps with **ough** words.

A visit to the circus

For my birthday, Nan th_____t

we _____t to visit the circus.

She b_____t our train tickets and we made our way

th_____ crowds of people.

Th_____we were tired later, we had had a wonderful

time.

Name

Objective: Spell words beginning with *br*, *cr*, *dr* and *fr*.

Brrr! It's freezing!

1. Join up the clues on the left to the **br** words in the box.

a colour

you use it to think

spans rivers and creeks
and harbours

used for sweeping floors;
also used by witches

a part of a tree

bridge

brown

branch

brain

broom

2. Match these clues to the **cr** words.

floats on top of milk

a big, black bird

to move very slowly

angry; also a shape like
this +

worn by kings and
queens

crown

cream

cross

crow

crawl

3. Now do the same with
these **dr** words.

a male duck

not wet

you have one when
you're thirsty

to die in water

it takes water away

drown

drake

drain

drink

dry

4. Match these clues to the **fr** words.

a day of the week

just picked or just
made

an animal that hops
and lives near water

the opposite of back

someone you like

front

Friday

fresh

friend

frog

Scholastic Literacy Skills
Spelling Ages 8–9

Photocopiable ▪ SCHOLASTIC Continued on P61

Name

Objective: Spell words beginning with *br, cr, dr, fr, gr* and *pr*.

Continued from P60

Unit 15

5. Match these clues to the **gr** words.

wheat, corn and barley are...

a colour

very big or very important

an insect

to complain

| grub |
| grumble |
| grains |
| green |
| great |

6. Match these clues to the **pr** words.

given when something is well done

to squeeze or flatten – a printing pr_____

good looking

she won first _____

used to hold things up

| prize |
| prop |
| praise |
| press |
| pretty |

7. Write any new words in your wordbank.

8. Use at least one of the words in each group to write a short story about a very cold day. Continue on the back of this sheet.

_____

_____

_____

_____

Name

- **Look** at these words.
- **Say** them aloud.
- **Cover** each set of words.
- **Write** them in your workbook.
- **Check** to see if you are right.

ferry foggy	funny carry	marry
cherry action	section portion	vision
television permission	swimming dripping	hopping
hoping hotter	wetter humming	chugging
Tuesday Wednesday	longer Friday	He's quite merry.
ought bought	thought through	enough

When you have written each set of words, CHECK them to see if they are right. If they are right, put a tick. If any are wrong, cross them out. Look carefully at the correct word(s) again, note where you went wrong and write them again in your wordbank.

There are 33 words. How many did you get right first time?

1. It was foggy when we crossed the River Mersey.

2. He watched television when he ought to have been working.

3. After swimming, he began coughing quite a bit.

4. They kicked their ball through his window, but said "Sorry."

5. She thought she ought to take me out.

6. He asked me, "Have you permission to go there?"

7. The water was very rough and she nearly drowned.

8. As the boat chugged along, the day became hotter and hotter.

9. They went to the station, but found a section had been closed.

Look at these sentences.

Say them aloud.

Cover each sentence.

Write them in your workbook.

Check to see if you are right.

Do the same with these sentences. (Don't forget to look at the punctuation!) You can WRITE, then CHECK after each sentence.

How many sentences were correct?

Enter any words that were not correct into your wordbank under the correct letter. Do this even if the word is there already.

What's cooking?

1. Read this aloud, then underline all the **oi**, **oa** and **ew** words.

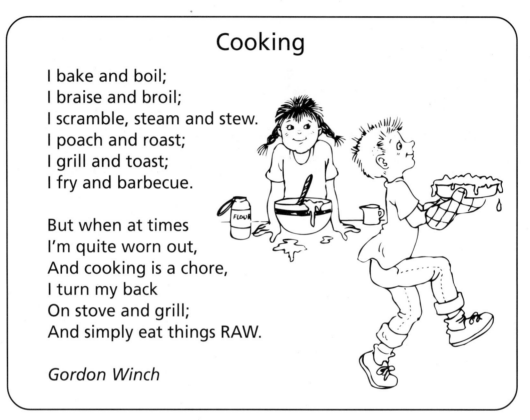

Cooking

I bake and boil;
I braise and broil;
I scramble, steam and stew.
I poach and roast;
I grill and toast;
I fry and barbecue.

But when at times
I'm quite worn out,
And cooking is a chore,
I turn my back
On stove and grill;
And simply eat things RAW.

Gordon Winch

2. Write any new words in your wordbank. Do you know what **braise** and **broil** mean? If not, use a dictionary to find out.

3. Here are some more **oi**, **oa** and **ew** words. Join the words that rhyme with a line.

> coil   crew   boat   coat   soil   few

4. Complete these words by filling in the spaces with the sound **oi**, **oa** or **ew**. Add any new words to your wordbank.

b____st   fl____t   fl____   ____ntment

p____son   c____st   d____   j____nt

thr____t   v____ce   b____t   n____

 Continued on P65

Name

Continued from P64

5. Write three sentences of your own, using an **oi**, **oa** or **ew** word in each sentence.

6. All these words begin with a consonant followed by **r**. Read the words aloud.

fry	grill	broil

When we say these words, the first two consonants are blended together. We call this a **consonant blend**.

7. Join the pairs of words that begin with the same consonant blend. The first one has been done for you.

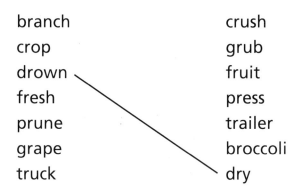

branch   crush
crop   grub
drown   fruit
fresh   press
prune   trailer
grape   broccoli
truck   dry

8. Write any new words in your wordbank. Remember to Look–Say–Cover–Write–Check the words.

9. What are your favourite foods? In your workbook, write about how you would make your favourite meal.

Name

Objective: Spell plurals of words ending in *o* or *oe* such as *potato* or *shoe*.

Unit 17

Singular or plural?

1. Read this story aloud.

> ### In our garden
> In our garden we grow potatoes, beans, peas and tomatoes. We always give some tomatoes to Grandma. We gave her two yesterday.
>
> Mum and Dad like fresh vegetables.
>
> "We would always eat fresh vegetables if we could," says Mum. "Our vegetables sometimes win prizes at the show and our tomatoes won a prize this year."
>
> "I would like to win a prize with my potatoes," says Dad.

2. Underline the **plural** words for **potato** and **tomato** in the story.

3. Complete the **plural** for each word below by adding **s** or **es**.

singular	plural
hero	*heroes*
potato	_____
tomato	_____
toe	*toes*
shoe	_____
oboe	_____
mango	_____
halo	_____
buffalo	_____
hoe	_____

Can you work out the rule?

Most words ending in **o** add **es** to make the plural.

Most words ending in **e** add **s** to make the plural.

4. Now Look–Say–Cover–Write each word in your wordbank. Remember to check!

Name

Objectives: Spell tricky plurals of words ending in *o*. Spell words ending in *oes*. Spell *of* and *off*.

Continued from P66

Unit **17**

Watch out for these unusual plurals! These words do not obey the rule because they come to us from different languages.

singular	**plural**
piano	pianos
cello	cellos
radio	radios
igloo	igloos
kangaroo	kangaroos

5. Write the words above in your wordbank. Use a dictionary to find out where the words come from.

The words **does** and **goes** also end in **oes**. These words are verbs. For example: Dad **does** the washing up every evening.

6. Read these sentences aloud. Can you hear the difference between **off** and **of**?

Skippy goes off with his friends.

Does Asha want a bag of crisps?

Of is pronounced **ov**.

When we say **off** we hear the **f** sound. **Off** is used to show movement.

7. Complete these sentences aloud, filling in the missing **off**, **of** or **oes** words.

Stacey g_____ to the shop to buy pota_____.

The t_____ fell _____ the table.

Which _____ these rad_____ is yours?

Mum's t_____ wiggle when she kicks _____ her

sh_____.

At the concert we heard flutes and ob_____.

Name

Objectives: Spell *ould* words. Recognise that some words come from the French language.

Unit **18**

A birthday treat

1. Read this story aloud. As you read, notice all the **ould** words.

A meal in a restaurant

On Dad's birthday, Mum said we could go to a restaurant for a meal. We set off early and arrived at the restaurant at half-past seven. All of us looked at the menu and decided what we would like.

Mum said she would like fish without potatoes. Dad ordered a steak and asked if he could have extra chips. Mark is a vegetarian so he ordered a broccoli bake. I had scampi and chips. Afterwards I ate a huge ice cream.

Later, I couldn't get to sleep. Perhaps I should not have eaten the ice cream!

2. Write the words **could**, **would** and **should** here.

Can you think of a way to remember **ould** words?

 One memory tip for **ould** words is to say

'**O U l**ucky **d**uck' when you write them.

3. Write all the **ould** words from the story into your wordbank. Write the memory tip sentence next to them if it helps your spelling.

 The French language can be seen and heard in many words to do with food and cooking. Some examples are **restaurant, menu** (meaning 'a list') and **café,** (meaning 'coffee').

4. Underline the words in the story above that are from the French language. Do you know any more words from French?

Continued from P68

Unit **18**

5. Read these tricky words aloud.

friend	busy	build	hear
tries	toilet	money	piece

6. Do you find any of these words difficult to spell? Look at these sentences. They may help you to remember how to spell them.

friend   I saw my friend on Friday.

busy   This bus is busy.

build   U and I build a house.

hear   I can hear with my ears.

tries   He tries and tries but he cannot kill flies.

money   He sat on a ton of money.

toilet   She did not spoil the toilet by pouring oil on it.

piece   Have a piece of pie.

7. Write the words that are tricky for you into your wordbank and next to each word write the memory tip sentence for it.

8. Make up some memory tip sentences of your own to help you with spellings which you find difficult. Funny ones are often the best.

_____

_____

_____

9. Write your memory tips in your wordbank next to the tricky words. Take care to check the spellings!

Name

Objective: Add *y* to nouns to make adjectives.

Foggy and frosty

1. Read these pairs of words aloud.

cream	steam	frost	grass
creamy	steamy	frosty	grassy

The words **cream**, **frost**, **steam** and **grass** are all **nouns**.

When we add **y** to these nouns we get words that describe **nouns**. We call these describing words **adjectives**.

For example: I put **cream** (noun) on my cornflakes.
My jumper is a **creamy** (adjective) colour.

2. Complete these sentences by changing nouns into adjectives.

It was so cold there was a frost.

It was a cold, fr_____ morning.

The grass needs cutting.

They ran down the gr_____ slope.

There was lots of steam in the kitchen.

The kitchen was very st_____ .

◼ SCHOLASTIC Continued on P71

Name

Objectives: Add *y* to nouns to make adjectives. Spell plurals of words ending in *f*.

Continued from P70 ————————————————————————————————— Unit **19**

3. Look at these pairs of words. Say them aloud.

noun	adjective
fog	foggy
bog	boggy
bag	baggy
sag	saggy
sun	sunny

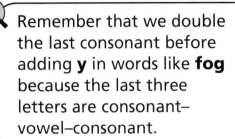

Remember that we double the last consonant before adding **y** in words like **fog** because the last three letters are consonant–vowel–consonant.

4. Write the five **adjectives** in your wordbank. Then write five sentences using the adjectives in your workbook.

5. Read these words aloud.

loaf	sheaf	leaf	hoof	thief
loaves	sheaves	leaves	hooves	thieves

When some words ending in **f** are made into plurals, we change the **f** to **v** before we add **es**.

Take care with these tricky plurals! They do not follow the rule.

singular	plural
roof	roofs
chief	chiefs
dwarf	dwarfs

Can you think of a way to remember these tricky plurals? This silly sentence may help you:

The dwarfs waved handkerchiefs from the roofs.

6. Write four sentences of your own in your workbook, using the plurals on this page. Here is one to start you off.

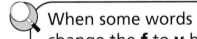

The baker makes lots of loaves.

Photocopiable 📖 S C H O L A S T I C

Scholastic Literacy Skills
Spelling Ages 8–9   **71**

Name

Objective: Add the suffixes *ed* and *ing* to verbs such as *cry*.

Cry, cried and crying

1. Say these words, then write them in your workbook.

cry	cried	crying
try	tried	trying
fry	fried	frying
dry	dried	drying

2. Write what happens when you add **ed** to a word like **cry**.

_____

3. Write what happens when you add **ing** to a word like **cry**.

_____

4. Add **ed** and **ing** to these **y** words, then write them down. The first one has been done for you.

reply	replied	replying
carry		
hurry		
marry		
pity		
ferry		
supply		

5. Write any new words in your wordbank.

72 Scholastic Literacy Skills
Spelling Ages 8–9

Photocopiable ■ SCHOLASTIC Continued on P73

Name

Objectives: Add the suffixes *ed* and *ing* to verbs such as *cry*. Use more interesting words than *got*, *nice* or *said*. Use the spelling pattern *ie* as in *chief* and *ei* as in *receive*.

Continued from P72

Unit 20

6. Now underline all the **y + ed** and **y + ing** words in these two sentences.

She pitied the child who had been crying.

He replied, "I am not supplying you with any more milk."

 We often use the words **got**, **nice** or **said** when we could find better words.

7. Rewrite these sentences in your workbook, changing **got**, **nice** or **said** for one of the words in the box.

I got a letter today.
He got on to the bus.
It was a nice day.
He said, "Are you ill?"
She said, "Help me!"

received	climbed	stepped
lovely	beautiful	asked
yelled	screamed	

ie or **ei**?

In many, but not all, **ie/ei** words, the **i** comes before the **e**. However, after the letter **c**, we nearly always put **e** before **i**.

Use this as a memory tip:

Have a p**ie**ce of p**ie**.

8. Read these words aloud, looking carefully at the **ie** or the **ei** in each of the words. Look up any words you don't know in the dictionary.

field	chief	brief	piece
receive	ceiling	deceive	

9. Write four sentences of your own, using **ie** or **ei** words. Add any new words to your wordbank.

Name

coin boil	coil coat	boat
boast throat	radio/radios piano/pianos	flew
piece busy	chief field	brief
potato potatoes	hero/heroes tomato/tomatoes	shoe/shoes
beautiful could	should steam/steamy	would
fog/foggy grass/grassy	leaf/leaves roof/roofs	loaf/loaves

Look at these words.

Say them aloud.

Cover each set of words.

Write them in your workbook.

Check to see if you are right.

When you have written each set of words, CHECK them to see if they are right. If they are right, put a tick. If any are wrong, cross them out. Look carefully at the correct word(s) again, note where you went wrong and write them again in your wordbank.

There are 40 words. How many did you get right first time?

Name

Continued from P74

1. Which one of you has eaten my fruit?

2. He replied, "I'm not carrying those loaves."

3. He tried to dry himself when he fell out of the boat.

4. You could help me to pick the tomatoes.

5. Would you come even if it is a foggy day?

6. I thought he might fall off the wall.

7. He did not receive the letter from his friend.

8. This bus is busy so I may walk to school.

9. The chief of police looked up at the ceiling.

10. She received a piece of pie from the waiter.

Look at these sentences.

Say them aloud.

Cover each sentence.

Write them in your workbook.

Check to see if you are right.

Do the same with these sentences. (Don't forget to look at the punctuation!) You can WRITE, then CHECK after each sentence.

How many sentences were correct?

Enter any words that were not correct into your wordbank under the correct letter. Do this even if the word is there already.

Name

Unit **21**

Sports mad

1. Read these sports words aloud.

> tennis   soccer   cricket   golf

2. Say the words in syllables. When you think you know them, write them in your wordbank.

> **tenn is   socc er   crick et   golf   bad min ton**

3. Many sports words are compound words. Write these four words.

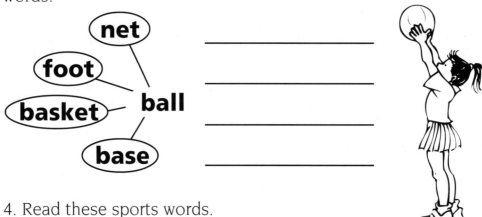

net
foot
basket **ball**
base

_____
_____
_____
_____

4. Read these sports words.

> sail   swim   skip
>
> jog   surf   run   ski

5. Now read them again, adding **ing** to each word. Write the words in your workbook.

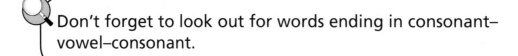

Don't forget to look out for words ending in consonant–vowel–consonant.

Objectives: Spell words in syllables. Add *ing* to words.

Continued from P76

Unit 21

6. Now split the sports words into syllables. One has already been done for you.

<u>surf ing</u>

When we add **ing** to verbs that end in **e**, we leave out the final **e**.

hik**e** —— (e)   hiking

7. Add **ing** to these words.

dance _____

dive _____

bike _____

hike _____

skate _____

8. Now write four sentences about your favourite sports, using some **ing** words.

_____

_____

_____

_____

_____

Name

Objectives: Revise some *ough* words.
Spell *ue* words as in *league*.

Unit **22**

Football facts

1. Read this text aloud.

Some facts about football

Football is a very old game. It is thought that the Chinese
played a kind of football about 2500 years ago.

The game has been played in Britain
for about 800 years. The old game was
very rough. Goal posts were often set
miles apart so the game went right
through the streets of towns or
villages. The players were tough and
many were badly hurt in football
fights. There were no rules.

In 1863 the Football Association was
formed and they decided there ought
to be rules. Later, clubs formed the
Football League. Notts County was
formed in 1862 and is the oldest club
in the League.

2. Look carefully at spellings which may be tricky for you,
especially the **ue** in leag**ue**.

3. Underline the **ough** words in the text.

4. In your workbook, write out an **ough** word family, using the
words you have underlined. Can you find any rhyming pairs?

5. Here are some other **ue** words. Read them aloud. Be careful!
The **ue** is not sounded in the first two.

> league   tongue   argue   barbecue   snooker cue

6. Write any new words in your wordbank. Remember to Look–
Say–Cover–Write–Check each word.

Name

Objective: Use the apostrophe to spell contractions such as *it's* and *I'll*.

Continued from P78

> **It's** is short for **it is** and **it has**.
>
> **It's** has been made shorter. That is why it is called a **contraction**.
>
> There are other contractions which you need to spell.
>
> **he's** is short for **he is** and **he has**.
>
> **I'll** is short for **I will**.

7. Rewrite these sentences, making the words underlined into contractions.

He is a good swimmer. _____

She is a good player. _____

I did not win the race. _____

What is the captain's name? _____

They cannot play today. _____

They have beaten us. _____

I will play netball with you. _____

8. These sentences have contractions. Write them again, changing the contractions into two words.

I'm ready to play football. _____

I've run all the way. _____

That's a good sport to play. _____

Don't miss the ball. _____

The sporting life

Some words start with two consonants. Here are two double consonant words with **l**:

black football boots   batting **gl**oves

1. Complete these sentences, filling in the spaces with the double consonants in the box below.

_____ow the whistle.

_____imb the rope.

Run _____at out.

_____oat in the pool.

Always wear sun_____asses at the beach.

cl	fl	gl	fl	bl

2. Complete the words in these sentences with **gl** or **cl**.

_____enn and _____oria _____ide down the hill on

their skis in the_____ean snow on a _____ear day.

How _____ever!

3. These words end in **mb**, but the **b** is not sounded. We call it a **silent b**. Read them aloud.

thumb	crumb	climb	dumb	comb	lamb

Name

Objectives: Spell words with *silent letters*. Distinguish between the homophones *no* and *know*.

 Continued from P80

Unit 23

4. Write six sentences, using **silent b**. Here is one to start you off.

"Don't climb too high!" Dad shouted.

5. Say these words aloud: **know   no**

Look carefully at the word **know**. It has a **silent k** and means something that we know with our mind. Words in the **know** family also have a **silent k**, for example **knowledge** and **knew**.

Know and **no** are **homophones**. They *sound* the same, but are spelled differently and have different meanings.

6. Complete these sentences, filling the spaces with **know**, **knew** or **knowledge**.

I don't kn_____ how to play tennis. Do you kn_____ the score?

He said he kn_____ the rules. She had no kn_____ of golf.

No can mean that we do not want to do something.
For example: **No, I will not go** ('I do not wish to go').
Or it can mean that we are without something.
For example: **I have no books** ('I do not have any books').
Remember that the prefix **non** also means 'no'.

7. Complete these sentences, using **no**, **non-** or **know**.

The skier had _____ money for new boots.

The sailor did not _____ the way home.

The sign says that _____ members are not welcome at the club.

" _____ ," she replied. "I didn't _____ that."

Objective: Distinguish between *it* and *its*.

It, its or it's?

 It is an easy word to spell. It can be in different parts of a sentence.

1. Read these sentences.

It is a tennis ball. Can you hit it?

Yes, I can play with it and hit it hard!

When **it** is used instead of a noun, we call it a **pronoun**.

2. Now read these sentences.

This is my tennis racquet.

Its frame is bent and its strings are broken.

 We use **its** when something is owned.

We do not spell **its** with an apostrophe (') if something is owned.

Its is a **possessive** pronoun.

3. Complete these sentences, filling the spaces with **it** or **its**.

I like tennis. Four people can play _____. You need to have a

tennis racket. _____ can be made of wood or other things.

_____ strings must be tight and _____ frame must not be

bent. _____ grip must not be too big for your hand. _____

head must not be too heavy or you will not be able to lift _____.

 Continued on P83

Objective: Distinguish between *its* and *it's*.

Continued from P82

Unit 24

It's is short for **it is** (and **it has**). We use an apostrophe with **its** only when it **means** 'it is'. (Remember an apostrophe means that a letter or letters have been left out.)

An easy way to test whether you use **its** or **it's** is to see if **it is** makes sense in the sentence. If it does, use **it's**.

For example: **It's (It is)** a game I like to play.

4. Complete these sentences, filling in the spaces with **its** or **it's**.

_____ winter and the snow is falling.

_____very thick and we can ski down the hill.

_____ fun to play cricket. _____ a good game to watch, too.

A cricket ball is hard. _____ leather cover is red.

5. Complete these sentences, filling in the spaces with **its** or **it's**.

_____ fun.

_____ colour is red.

_____ rules are hard.

_____ good to go skating.

Have you seen _____ cover?

_____ time to go swimming.

_____ the winning team.

_____ sailing that I like best.

_____ motor was running.

Objectives: Distinguish between the spellings and meanings of *there, their* and *theirs*.

Unit 25

There, there...

1. **Their** and **there** are **homophones**. Do you know what that means?

_____

_____

There often means a place. For example: I put it **there**.

Their is a possessive pronoun (like **its**) and means something belonging to them. For example: **Their** mother was good.

If you get **there** and **their** mixed up, try seeing the word **here** in the word t**here**. It may help you to remember that **there** often means a place. You could make up a memory tip too, using the words **here** and **there**.

Theirs is used in the same way as **their** and means something belonging to them. For example: That book is **theirs**.

2. Finish these sentences, filling the spaces with **there**, **their**, or **theirs**. Write any new words in your wordbank.

_____ favourite sport is swimming.

They played tennis over _____ by the wall.

_____ golf shots are good.

Mine are rubbish. _____ go near the hole.

My favourite sport is jogging, _____ is hiking.

They put _____ dirty football sweaters _____ by the chair.

 Continued on P85

Name

Look carefully at the tricky word **favourite**. If it is tricky for you, try splitting it into three syllables: **fav our ite**. Can you see the word **our** in **favourite**?

Here is a memory tip sentence for **favourite**:

Our fav**our**ite word is fav**our**ite!

3. Maybe you do not like sport, or are not very good at it. This is a poem about a boy who is left until last when teams are picked. Is that you? Read the poem aloud.

Picking teams

When we pick teams in the playground,
Whatever the game might be,
There's always somebody left till last
And usually it's me.

I stand there looking hopeful
And tapping myself on the chest,
But the captains pick the others first,
Starting, of course, with the best.

Maybe if teams were sometimes picked
Starting with the worst,
Once in his life a boy like me
Could end up being first!

Allan Ahlberg

4. Now find examples of the following in the poem above and underline them:

- one **compound word**
- one **double consonant + ing**
- two **contractions**
- a word in the **ould** family
- a word in the **one** family
- one word with the **suffix ful**.

Name _____

Look at these words.

Say them aloud.

Cover each set of words.

Write them in your workbook.

Check to see if you are right.

netball	swimming	running
football	jogging	
bike/biking	dive/diving	skip/skipping
hike/hiking	dance/dancing	
league	tongue	argue
barbecue	snooker cue	
arguing	didn't	float
can't	blow	
sunglasses	comb	lamb
climb	thumb	
its tail	their mother	favourite
its tongue	their house	

When you have written each set of words, CHECK them to see if they are right. If they are right, put a tick. If any are wrong, cross them out. Look carefully at the correct word(s) again, note where you went wrong and write them again in your wordbank.

There are 40 words. How many did you get right first time?

 Continued on P87

Name

Continued from P86

1. She's swimming for the school tonight.

2. The Football League was formed over 100 years ago.

3. It is thought that the Chinese were the first to play football.

4. We know they are going to climb that mountain.

5. Do you know if their snooker cues are broken?

6. Their combs had been put over there near the table.

7. The little girl looked at the dog and then patted its head.

8. My favourite sports in July and August are jogging and diving.

9. Their throats were sore so their voices were quiet.

10. "Would you help me?" he asked quite quietly.

Look at these sentences.

Say them aloud.

Cover each sentence.

Write them in your workbook.

Check to see if you are right.

Do the same with these sentences. (Don't forget to look at the punctuation!) You can WRITE, then CHECK after each sentence.

How many sentences were correct?

Enter any words that were not correct into your wordbank under the correct letter. Do this even if the word is there already.

Name

Using a dictionary

A dictionary is a book of words and their meanings, set out in alphabetical order. To use a dictionary quickly, you need to know the order of letters in the alphabet.

1. Say the alphabet aloud quickly to check you know the order.

When you look up a word in a dictionary, you don't have to turn each page to find a word. If the word begins with any letter from **a** to **i**, you will find it near the *beginning* of the dictionary. If the word begins with any letter from **j** to **r**, you will find it *somewhere in the middle*. Words that begin with letters from **s** to **z** will be *near the end*.

2. Read this list of words. They are all types of clothes. See how quickly you can find the words in a dictionary. Time yourself if you can. As soon as you have found one word, move on quickly to the next. The words are in alphabetical order to help you.

anorak   cap   gloves   jeans   sweater   trainers

3. Write all the words in your wordbank. Remember to use Look–Say–Cover–Write–Check for each word.

If two words begin with the same letter, you have to look at the second letter of each word to see which comes first in the dictionary.

For example: **sock** comes before **sweater** in the dictionary because **o** comes before **w** in the alphabet.

  Continued on P89

Name

Objectives: Know alphabetical order. Use dictionaries.

4. Read these clothes words aloud. Then cover the words up and write them in the spaces. Check spellings very carefully.

vest _____   skirt _____

tie _____   shoes _____

pyjamas _____   boots _____

trainers _____   pullover _____

anorak _____   slippers _____

5. Now number the list of words from 1 to 10 in alphabetical order, beginning: **1. anorak**.

6. Write the words again, this time in alphabetical order. Check that each word is spelled correctly and that it is in the correct place.

_____

_____

_____

_____

_____

Objective: Spell words containing consonant blends and digraphs.

Smelly socks

Some words, like **bl**ue or **gl**oves, start with two consonant sounds. These are called **consonant blends**.

1. Complete these clothes words, adding one of these consonant blends: **sl**, **tr**, **sw**, **dr** or **gl**.

_____ippers   _____ainers   _____oves

_____acks   _____eater   _____ess

Some words start with two consonants which make *one* sound.

Two examples are **sh** and **th**.

We call these **digraphs**. **Digraph** comes from two Greek words – **dis** (which means 'twice') and **graphe** (which means 'writing').

2. Complete these words, adding a **sh** or **th** digraph to each one.

_____ough   _____orts   _____op

3. Write four sentences of your own, using the words you have made. Here is one to start you off.

My brother has got new trainers.

Consonant blends and digraphs can come at the ends of words:

She came fir<u>st</u> in the fancy dress parade – **st** is a consonant blend at the end of a word.

He came fif<u>th</u> in the race – **th** is a digraph at the end of a word.

Photocopiable **SCHOLASTIC** Continued on P91

4. Finish these sentences, filling each space with a consonant blend or a digraph. Then circle the consonant blends and underline the digraphs.

These runners came fir_____, seco_____, thi_____, four_____,

fif_____, six_____, seven_____, eigh_____, nin_____, ten_____.

5. Now do the same with this poem. **ck** is a digraph too.

Jock's socks

Jo_____'s so_____s smell,

Jo_____'s so_____s pong.

Jo_____'s had them on

Far too lo_____.

Gregory Blaxell

Did you remember to circle the consonant blend in **po<u>ng</u>**?

6. Read these words aloud. They are arranged in word families. Underline the family parts.

though	shop	dress	long	fourth
thick	shorts	drink	gong	fifth
think	shout	drill	song	sixth

7. Use your dictionary to find three more words beginning with the **th** digraph and three beginning with the **sh** digraph. Add them to the word families above.

Knights in armour

1. Say these **silent k** words. Write any new words in your wordbank.

knife   knob   knee   knit   knot   knock   knapsack

2. Complete these sentences, filling in the spaces using **silent k** words.

My mother will _____ me a sweater.

The _____ wore a suit of armour.

I went hiking with a _____ on my back.

His socks came up to his _____.

3. Say these words aloud. Take care to sound the letter **h** and circle it – this will help you to spell it.

why   when   which   where   while   whip

4. Finish these sentences, filling each space with a **silent k** word or a **wh** word.

_____en will you finish _____nitting my _____ite sweater?

_____ere are my trainers?

_____y did you _____nock on the door?

_____ich shorts will you wear _____ile you are running?

Continued on P93

Name

Objectives: Spell words with *silent k*.
Distinguish between silent letter
homophones such as *knot* and *not*.
Distinguish between *of* and *off*.

Continued from P92

5. Don't forget that the verbs **know** and **knew** begin with a **silent
k**. Write two sentences of your own, using **know** and **knew**.

_____

_____

6. Say these sentences aloud, then underline the homophones.

He threw the ball through the window.

There is no shirt here. I do not know where it is.

The little boy was so frightened he let out a wail when he saw
the whale.

Which is the good witch and which is the bad witch?

7. Complete this sentence with the correct **homophone** for each
space.

A (knight/night) _____ (would/wood) _____ (knot/

not) _____ (where/wear) _____ his armour to bed

at (knight/night) _____, (wood/would) _____ he?

Of and **off** are *not* homophones, but they almost look the
same.

8. Using **of** and **off**, complete and write these sentences.

He picked one _____ his ties out _____ the bag.

He fell _____ his bike and ran _____ crying.

Name

Objectives: Revise *you're* and *your*.
Revise *they're* and *their*. Revise alphabetical
order.

Remember, remember!

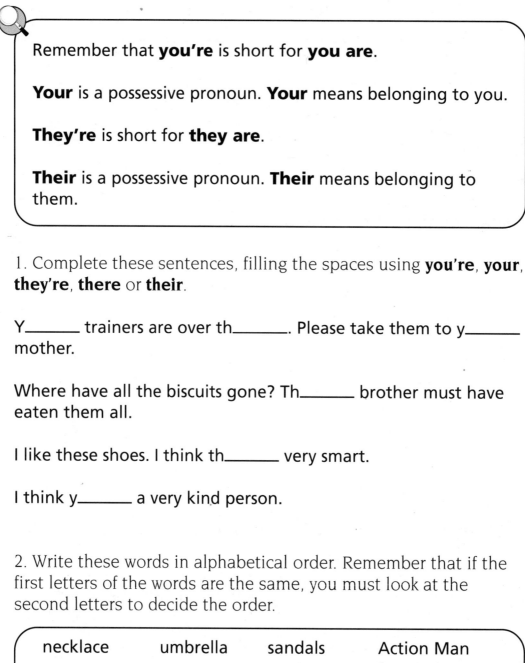

Remember that **you're** is short for **you are**.

Your is a possessive pronoun. **Your** means belonging to you.

They're is short for **they are**.

Their is a possessive pronoun. **Their** means belonging to them.

1. Complete these sentences, filling the spaces using **you're**, **your**, **they're**, **there** or **their**.

Y_____ trainers are over th_____. Please take them to y_____ mother.

Where have all the biscuits gone? Th_____ brother must have eaten them all.

I like these shoes. I think th_____ very smart.

I think y_____ a very kind person.

2. Write these words in alphabetical order. Remember that if the first letters of the words are the same, you must look at the second letters to decide the order.

| necklace | umbrella | sandals | Action Man |
| station | blouse | underpants | nation |

_____

_____

▲SCHOLASTIC Continued on P95

Name

Continued from P94

Syllables can help you to spell: you spell the words in parts; you hear the parts as you say the words, like this:

stock ing   trou sers   sing let

3. Read this poem aloud and divide words with two syllables like this: **trou / sers**.

Simon's Singlet

Simon's special singlet
Had stripes of green and white.
Simon liked his singlet;
He wore it day and night.

When Simon tried to slip it off
To go in for a swim,
He found his special singlet
Had become a part of him.

Gordon Winch

5. Do you know what a **singlet** is? Look up the meaning in your dictionary and write it here.

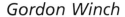

6. Did you notice the tricky spelling **spe<u>ci</u>al** in the poem? Here are some more **ci** words. Read them aloud very carefully. They are tricky!

facial   precious

delicious   suspicious

 The last four letters of **special** sound like **shal** and the **ci** sounds like **sh**.

7. Find out the meaning of the **ci** words you do not know by looking them up in your dictionary. Now Look–Say–Cover–Write the words in your wordbank. Remember to check!

Objective: Spell words with *ish*.

Sort of brown

A **brownish** coat is one that is sort of brown, or a little bit brown. In this poem the colours are brownish.

1. Read the poem aloud.

Sort of brown

Most things aren't any real colour
in my town;
they're sort of brown,
like dust and dead leaves
and sleeves
that have been on people
for a day or two.
Most things aren't red or green
or yellow or blue;
they're sort of brown
I think.
Don't you?

Gordon Winch

2. Make these colours in the clothes here 'sort of' by adding **ish**. Don't forget that 'sort of' red must have two **d**s. What happens to the **e** in blue?

green sweater_____   black trousers _____

red shirt   _____   grey skirt   _____

yellow tie   _____   blue socks   _____

3. Describe three of your favourite clothes in your workbook. Think about their colours and when you might wear them. When you have some ideas, use them to write a short poem.

Name

continued from P96

4. Read these words, adding the suffix **er** to each one. Write the new word next to them.

kick _____

slip _____

wide _____

sweat_____

diver _____

run _____

When we add the suffix **er** to words, some roots of words stay the same.

train + er   train**er**

When we add the suffix **er** to words that end in **e** we just add **r** because the **e** is there already.

ride + er   rid**er**

When we add the suffix **er** to short words that end in a single consonant, we double the consonant.

hat + er   hatt**er**

5. Say all the **er** words you can make from these roots. Then write the **er** words.

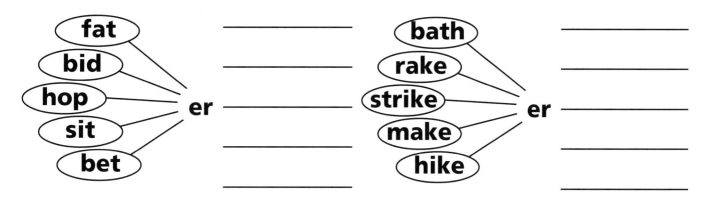

6. Read these sentences, filling the spaces with the suffix **er** or **ers**. Write the finished sentences in your workbook.

He is the best kick_____ in the team when he wears his

train_____.

Dad wears his slipp_____ at night.

I wear a glove if I am the catch_____.

The bath_____ are in the water.

Name

Look at these words.

Say them aloud.

Cover each set of words.

Write them in your workbook.

Check to see if you are right.

trainers skirt	sweater slippers	gloves
first eighth	though thick	fourth
knife knock	knees why	where
which when	He threw his ball. She looked through the window.	night
You're late! They're out.	their dog It's there.	your friend
red/reddish blue/bluish	special delicious	hiker

When you have written each set of words, CHECK them to see if they are right. If they are right, put a tick. If any are wrong, cross them out. Look carefully at the correct word(s) again, note where you went wrong and write them again in your wordbank.

There are 45 words. How many did you get right first time?

Name

Continued from P98

review (Units 26–30)

1. Where is your new pullover?

2. Are you too hot? If so, take off your sweater.

3. I should have put on my favourite anorak.

4. He knew that my slippers were too small for him.

5. That is the fourth time I've fallen off the wall.

6. I do not know where my hiking boots are.

7. The knight shouted, "Stop that silly crying!"

8. You're not going to eat all my delicious fruit.

9. He could never have pulled the nail out of the rough wood.

10. My favourite month is February as long as it's not too cold.

Look at these sentences.

Say them aloud.

Cover each sentence.

Write them in your workbook.

Check to see if you are right.

Do the same with these sentences. (Don't forget to look at the punctuation!) You can WRITE, then CHECK after each sentence.

How many sentences were correct?

Enter any words that were not correct into your wordbank under the correct letter. Do this even if the word is there already.

Name

Aa
abode
action
Action Man
afraid
aid
aim
alone
anorak
are
argue
arguing
asked
ate

Bb
bad
baddy
bag
ball
barbecue
baseball
basketball
bat
be
beach
beating
beautiful
being
bike
biking
black
blouse
blue
bluish
boast
boat
bog

boil
bone
boots
bought
brain
branch
bridge
brief
broccoli
broil
broom
brown
buffalo
build
busy
buy
by

Cc
camping
can't
cap
caravan
carry
catch
caught
ceiling
chalk
cheerful
cherry
chief
chiefs
chug
chugging
claim
clean
cleanest
cleaning

climb
climbed
coat
code
coil
coin
comb
complain
cone
could
crawl
cream
creamy
creep
crept
crew
cried
crop
cross
crow
crown
crumb
crush
cry
crying

Dd
dad
daddy
dance
dancing
deceive
deckchair
delicious
didn't
die
dim
dip

dive
diving
does
dog
doing
dome
drain
drake
dress
dried
drill
drink
drip
dripped
dripping
drive
drove
drown
drum
dry
drying
dumb
dwarf
dwarfs
dye

Ee
eat
eighth
enough
explode
eye

Ff
facial
fail
faithless
fan

fanned
fanning
fat
fatter
fattest
favourite
February
fed
feed
feel
felt
ferry
few
fiction
field
fifth
first
fit
flew
float
fly
fog
foggy
football
fought
fourth
free
freedom
freeing
fresh
Friday
fried
friend
frog
front
frost
frosty
fruit

Continued from P100

wordbank

fry
frying
fun
funny
furry

Gg
gate
gateway
gloves
goes
gong
goodbye
grains
grape
grass
grassy
great
green
grey
grill
grub
grumble

Hh
halo
hear
her
hero
heroes
hike
hiking
his
hoe
holidays
home
honey
hoof

hooves
hop
hoping
hopped
hopping
hot
hotter
house
hug
hugged
hugging
hum
human
humming
hurry

Ii
ice cream
igloo
igloos
it

Jj
jeans
Jenny
Jock
jog
jogging

Kk
kangaroo
knapsack
knee
knees
knew
knife
knit
knob

knock
knot
know

Ll
lamb
leaf
league
leaves
lie
livestock
loaf
loaves
long
lotion
lovely

Mm
maid
main
mango
marry
me
meet
member
mention
merry
met
mist
misty
money
mother

Nn
nail
nation
national
necklace

netball
new
night
ninth
no
nod
non-member
non-payment
nonsense
non-slip
non-stick
non-stop
not
nought

Oo
oboe
of
off
ought
our

Pp
packing
pain
paint
painted
painter
pat
patted
patting
payment
penny
permission
phone
piano
pianos
pie

piece
pies
pin
pinned
pinning
pity
plane
portion
potato
potatoes
praise
precious
prefer
preferred
press
pretty
prevention
prize
prop
provision
prune
pullover
pup
puppy
pyjamas

Qq
quarry
quiet
quite

Rr
radio
radios
rain
raise
receive
received

Name

wordbank

red
reddish
relation
remain
replied
reply
replying
rig
rocket
rode
Rome
roof
roofs
rough
run
running
runny
rye

Ss
sag
sail
sailor
sandals
scene
scenery
scent
scented
science
scientist
scissors
screamed
scythe
sea
seaside
second
section
seize

sense
seventh
she
sheaf
sheaves
shelf
shelves
shirt
shoe
shoes
shorts
should
shout
silly
sit
sixth
skate
ski
skiing
skip
skipping
skirt
sleep
slept
slip
slippers
smoking
snooker cue
socks
soil
song
Spain
span
special
station
steam
steamy
stepped

stick
stone
stop
sun
sunglasses
sunny
sunshine
supply
surf
surfing
suspicious
sweater
swim
swimming

Tt
tail
talked
tan
tanned
tanner
tanning
telephone
television
tenth
their
theirs
them
there
they
thick
thief
thieves
think
third
thong
though
thought

throat
through
thumb
ticket
tie
Timmy
to
toe
toes
toilet
tomato
tomatoes
Tommy
tone
tongue
too
tough
trailer
train
trainers
tried
tries
trousers
truck
try
trying
Tuesday
tummy

Uu
umbrella
underpants
unfaithful
unlucky
us

Vv
very
vest
vision
visitor

Ww
wag
walk
walked
Wednesday
wet
wetter
what
when
where
which
while
whip
why
would

Yy
yelled
yellow
you
your

Zz
zap

Name

Objective: Spell words with the *a* sound as in *pain*.

Supplementary unit 1 See Unit 1 **pages 28–9**

Building sandcastles

1. Write the **ain** words in the sandcastles.

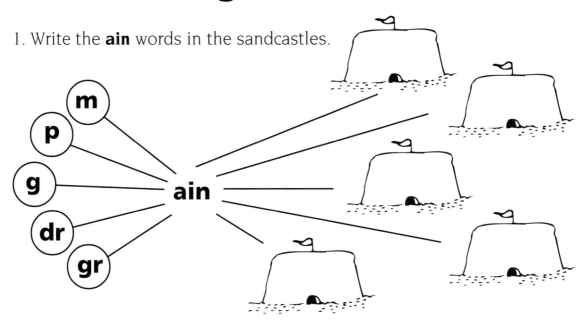

m
p
g
dr
gr
ain

2. Now write two sentences below, using some of the **ain** words.

_____

_____

3. Write the **ail** words in the sandcastles.

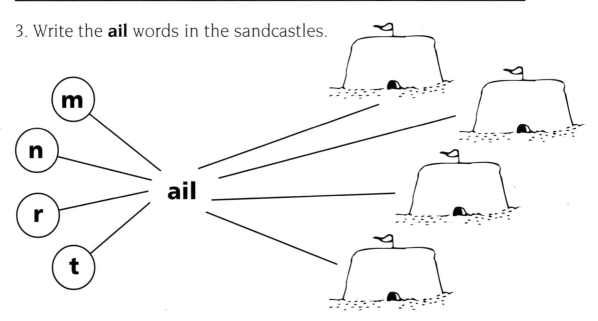

m
n
r
t
ail

4. Now write two sentences below, using some of the **ail** words.

_____

_____

Name

Objective: Spell words with the _a_ sound as in _raise_.

Continued from P28 Supplementary unit **2** See Unit 1 **pages 28–9**

Fishing for 'a' words

1. Finish these sentences, using **aim**, **ait** or **ais** words from the box.

> raise   bait   claimed   wait   praised

I used a worm as b_____.

I can't w_____ till Christmas.

Who c_____ the money that was found?

Her piano playing was p_____ by the judges.

We r_____ the flag every Monday morning.

2. Write the **ail**, **ain** or **ait** words around the square. They should all have an **a** sound as in **bait**.

br	st	gr
pl	ain ail ait	tr
fr		sl

3. Use some of the words in two sentences of your own.

_____

_____

Name

Supplementary unit **3** See Unit 2 **page 30**

To, two and too

To, **two** and **too** are all tricky words to spell. They sound the same but have different meanings and spellings.

to   We went **to** the beach **to** swim.

too   Grandma came **too**.

two   Our holiday lasted for **two** weeks.

1. Write the correct word – **to**, **too** or **two** – in the sentences below.

We went _____ the shops and bought _____ apples.

She has _____ brothers.

Mum gave me some money and she gave

some _____ my sister _____.

Are you going _____ play with me?

They have some bread and some cakes _____.

James is in the garden and the baby is there _____.

I cannot eat _____ ice creams.

Please help me _____ open this box.

Objective: Spell words with the suffixes
less and *ful*.

Supplementary unit **4** See Unit 3 **page 33**

Fearless and hopeful

The suffix **less** means 'without'.
For example: **He is friend<u>less</u>** means 'he is without friends'.

The suffix **ful** means 'having'.
For example: **She is hope<u>ful</u>** means 'she has hope'.

1. Add the suffix **less** to these words.

end _____   fear _____

tire _____   hope _____

care _____   friend _____

2. Now use each word in a sentence of your own.

_____

_____

_____

_____

_____

_____

3. Do the same with these six words – but add the suffix **ful**. Write
your sentences on the back of this sheet.

sorrow _____   joy _____

care _____   fear _____

hope _____   play _____

Syllables and suffixes

1. Make two-syllable words from these one-syllable words by adding a suffix such as **ing**, **less** or **ful**.

train _____

fail _____

brain _____

pain _____

rain _____

2. Say these words. Listen to the syllables. Look at the words and parts of the words. Divide the words into their syllables.

packing _____ _____

deckchair _____ _____

dockyard _____ _____

rocket _____ _____

lucky _____ _____

hanging _____ _____

wingless _____ _____

matches _____ _____

seeing _____ _____

began _____ _____

seaside _____ _____

beating _____ _____

Name

Supplementary unit **6** See Unit 5 **page 36**

Irregular past tenses

When we change verbs into the past tense, we add **ed** or **d**.

For example: I talk**ed**   We chatt**ed**   She hear**d**

But some past tenses are irregular.

1. Say these verbs aloud. They are all unusual past tenses.

gave	caught	felt	grew	swam
thought	bought	came	threw	dug

2. Write the verbs that make sense in the spaces in the story.

On my holidays I _____ in the sea and _____

in the sand. After a while, I _____ a bit chilly and so I

_____ I would have a hot drink. My Dad _____

me some money and I _____

a drink at the shop on the beach. I

_____ warmer very quickly.

My brother had been fishing and

_____ a little fish. It was so

small that he _____ it back

into the water.

Name

Objective: Spell *our*, *are* and *or*.

Supplementary unit **7** See Unit 5 **page 37**

Going on holiday

1. Say these sentences slowly and carefully so that you can hear the differences in the sounds of the words: **our**, **are** and **or**.

> **Our** means 'belonging to us': **Our** house is nice.
>
> **Are** is a verb: They **are** in the car.   We **are** going home.
>
> **Or** usually means that we can choose something else:
>
> Shall I eat now **or** later?   I could paint in green **or** yellow.

2. Write **our**, **are** or **or** in this story so that it makes sense.

We _____ going on holiday soon in _____ caravan.

I don't know whether to take my blue jeans _____ my

black ones. If the weather is good, we _____ hoping to

have lots of picnics on the beach. Aunt Nancy will look after

_____ cat. I wonder if we will travel at night _____

early in the morning?

Photocopiable **SCHOLASTIC**

Scholastic Literacy Skills
Spelling Ages 8–9

109

Name

Don't cry!

1. Make **y** and **ye** words.

Write them here. _____   _____

_____   _____   _____

_____   _____   _____

2. Read these sentences aloud.
Fill in the spaces with the **y** or **ye**
words that make sense.

A _____ fox crept into the pig _____.

_____ flour makes delicious bread.

I stood _____ the door and waved _____ to Dad.

The red _____ from the paper came off on _____ hands.

"Don't _____," she said to the sad boy.

Name

Painting a scene

1. All the words in the box have a **silent c**. Read the story and fill in the spaces with the word that makes sense. Look at them carefully. Try to write them from memory. Don't copy!

> scent   scissors   scythe   scientist   science   scene

As I walked in the country, I could smell the _____ of

hay. An old farmer was cutting his hay with a _____. It

was a lovely _____. "I will paint that," I said to myself.

When I arrived back

home, my sister was

busy doing her

_____

homework. (She wants

to be a _____

when she is older!) I

used her

_____ to cut

out paper for my

painting.

Name

Objective: Spell words with the vowel *o* and *magic e*.

Supplementary unit 10 See Unit 8 **pages 44–5**

When in Rome...

1. Read the following silly poem and fill in the spaces with words from the box.

Rome   home   explode   abode

(Check the meaning of **abode** in your dictionary.)

I'm here in _____,

But I have no _____.

The fact is I have no _____.

Won't somebody give me a place to live

Or I think I shall _____!

2. Now write the poem on the back of this sheet. Try to do it from memory – so learn the poem first. (Don't forget to look at the punctuation too.)

3. Draw a funny picture to go with it.

Scholastic Literacy Skills
Spelling Ages 8–9
112

Photocopiable ♦SCHOLASTIC

Name

Your and you're

> **Your** is used when we mean something belongs to you:
> **Your** book is here.
>
> **You're** is short for **you are**: **You're** late.
>
> (The apostrophe shows where the letter **a** has been left out.)
>
> Remember, if you are not sure, try to say 'you are' and, if it makes sense, use **you're**. If it doesn't, use **your**.

1. Write **your** or **you're** in the following five sentences.

Y_____ making me laugh
with all those silly stories.

Y_____ friend is here.

Is that y_____ idea of a joke?

They said y_____ going to a party.

I think y_____ too late for dinner.

2. Now write two sentences of your own using **your** and **you're**.

_____

_____

_____

_____

Name

Objective: Spell *tion* words.

At the station

tion – these four letters sound like **shun**.

1. Say these eight **tion** words aloud. Look at them carefully, and write them from memory. Don't copy! It may help if you divide them into syllables as you write them.

(Check the meanings of any words you don't already know.)

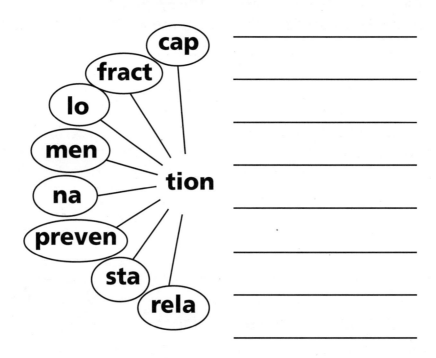

2. Make up four sentences of your own using four of these **tion** words. Here is one to start you off.

The station was closed because of the snow.

_____

_____

_____

_____

Name

Supplementary unit **13** See Unit 10 **page 49**

Two meanings of 'too'

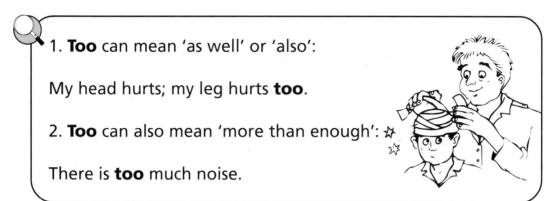

1. **Too** can mean 'as well' or 'also':

My head hurts; my leg hurts **too**.

2. **Too** can also mean 'more than enough':

There is **too** much noise.

1. In these sentences write in the brackets either **1** or **2** to show which meaning of **too** has been used.

This puzzle is too (   ) tricky.

I think the clock is too (   ) fast now.

David came to my house and Shaun came too. (   )

Cathy and Marianne were too (   ) full to eat any more.

Keith went to the football match, and Rick went too. (   )

The two boys were laughing too (   ) much to hear Mum call them.

2. Now write two sentences of your own, using the two meanings of **too**.

_____

_____

_____

_____

Name

Objective: Spell words with the *i* sound as in *cherry*. Double the last consonant in CVC words before adding *y*.

Supplementary unit **14** See Units 11 & 13 **pages 52–3 & 57–8**

Christmas

1. Use the words in the box to finish these sentences.

> tummy   carry   chatty   merry   runny

We had a very _____ Christmas.

I don't feel well – my _____ hurts.

This cold has given me a _____ nose.

Can I _____ your bag?

Our neighbour is very _____.

Write any new words in your wordbank.

 Dan is a one-syllable word. **Danny** is a two-syllable word.

2. Look at the words below. Add **y** to each one. Then divide each word into two syllables. The first one has been done for you.

Dan   *Dan ny*

Len   _____

Ben   _____

gran _____

fun   _____

tin   _____

pen   _____

 The last three letters of each one are consonant–vowel–consonant.

In words like these we double the last consonant before adding **y**.

Name

Danny's book

1. Read this little play and circle every **his**.

DANNY: It's my book.

SISTER: No it's not. That book's mine.

DAD: If it's his, give it back to him.

SISTER: But it's not. It's mine. He just says it's his.

DAD: If he said it's his, it's his. Give it back.

SISTER: You're not fair. Here, have the book.

(She throws it down on the floor.)

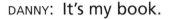

2. Use **he**, **him** or **his** to finish these sentences.

_____ is always on Danny's side.

He can keep _____ rotten book.

I won't ever lend _____ a book again.

He's awful. He keeps saying it's _____.

3. Write three sentences of your own, using **he**, **him** and **his**.

_____

_____

_____

Name

What's on television?

sion is a suffix which sounds like **shun**.

(Remember that **tion** sounds like **shun** too!)

1. Use the correct **sion** word in the spaces in these sentences.
Choose your words from the box.

television	permission
diversion	vision
decision	collision

The man had poor _____ and had to wear very strong glasses.

Dad gave me _____ to watch _____ when my homework was finished.

There was a _____ sign in the road, so Mum had to drive home another way.

The accident involved a _____ between a car and a lorry.

The jury made the _____ that she was innocent.

2. Write any new words in your wordbank.

Name

Objective: Spell *ough* and *ought* words.

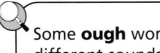

Supplementary unit 17 See Unit 14 **pages 58–9**

That's enough!

Some **ough** words sound alike (rhyme), but others have different sounds.

1. Read aloud the sentences below. Join the **ough** words that rhyme. Take care – some words cannot be put into a rhyming pair.

The sea was very **rough**.

He **thought** I was ill.

I looked **through** the window.

The **bough** on the tree broke.

She **bought** a cake.

The meat was quite **tough**.

I went out even **though** it was raining.

I **ought** to go home.

2. Write the **ough** or **ought** word which makes sense in these six sentences.

nought   though   through   thought   enough   fought

They _____ like cat and dog.

I have had _____ pudding, thank you.

I put a _____ on 10 and made it into 100.

She climbed to the top, even _____ she was tired.

She _____ it was time to go home.

They made their way _____ the crowd of people.

Photocopiable ■SCHOLASTIC

Scholastic Literacy Skills
Spelling Ages 8–9 **119**

Name

Objective: Spell words that contain *r* in
their initial consonant blend.

Supplementary unit **18** See Unit 15 **pages 60–1**

Growing grapes in Australia (1)

1. Read these instructions about growing grapes. (Check the
meanings of any words you don't know such as **vine**, **pruned** and
creek.) Circle each word that has a consonant and then an **r** at
the beginning. The first one has been done for you.

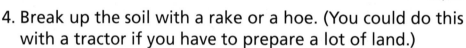

(Gr)owing grapes in Australia

Preparing the ground
1. Choose ground away from trees.

2. Dig up, removing all the grass.

3. Make sure the ground is well drained.

4. Break up the soil with a rake or a hoe. (You could do this
   with a tractor if you have to prepare a lot of land.)

Planting the grape vines
5. Run a line across the ground to keep the vines in rows.

6. Dig a hole for each vine. You could use a trowel for this.
   The holes should be two metres apart.

7. Put the pruned vine into the hole and spread out the
   roots.

8. Use water from the creek to give each vine a drink.

9. Fill in the hole.

10. Trample the soil firmly around each vine.

2. Now write all the words you have circled in your wordbank.

Scholastic Literacy Skills
Spelling Ages 8–9

Photocopiable **SCHOLASTIC**

Name

(**Supplementary unit** 19) See Unit 15 **pages 60–1**

Growing grapes in Australia (2)

1. Write down all the words that begin with a consonant followed by an **r** in the text 'Growing grapes in Australia'.

_____   _____   _____

_____   _____   _____

_____   _____   _____

_____   _____   _____

2. Join the words on the right that begin with the same **consonant blend** (two consonants).

branch	crush
crop	fruit
drown	grub
fresh	press
grain	trailer
prize	broccoli
truck	dry

3. Make words from the grid below that begin with a **consonant blend** that contains **r**. The first one has been done for you.

_____*bride*_____

_____

_____

_____

_____

_____

_____

br	cr	dr
gr	-ide -ain -ane -ame	pr
tr		fr

Objective: Spell *oi*, *oa* and *ew* words.

Supplementary unit **20** See Unit 16 **pages 64–5**

Oi!

1. Choose the correct **oi** word from the box to finish these sentences. Write any new **oi** words in your wordbank.

> oil   point   soil   ointment   spoil   coin

The _____ on my pencil is not sharp enough.

The nurse put some _____ on my leg.

I think this _____ is worth 50p.

The car needs some _____.

Is there _____ on your wellingtons?

Will the rain _____ my new sweater?

2. Write the **oa** and **ew** words in the spaces. Say them aloud as you write.

b   c   fl   g   m   thr   **oat** _____

br   cr   d   f   fl   gr   n   s   **ew** _____

Name

One potato, two potatoes

Most words ending in **o** become plural by adding **es**:
potato   potato**es**.

Those ending in **oe** just add **s**: toe toe**s**.

Words ending in **y** change the **y** to **i** and add **es**:
baby   bab**ies**.

1. Write the correct plural word in the sentences below. Put new spellings into your wordbank – but don't just copy!

They were having (potato) _____, (tomato)

_____ and (cherry) _____ for their dinner.

They visited many (factory) _____ when they were in

the big (city) _____.

My (shoe) _____ were tight and my (toe)

_____ were hurting.

We had a ride on two (lorry)

_____.

They said the soldiers were

(hero) _____.

Grandma and Grandad like to
tell me about their (memory)

_____ of childhood.

(Supplementary unit 22) See Unit 17 **page 67**

Off she goes!

Say **of** aloud – it sounds like **ov**.

Say **off** aloud – you should hear the **f** sound in it. **Off** usually means there is movement: He **fell off** the wall.

Does and **goes** are not plural nouns; they are verbs.

Say them aloud – they sound different.

1. Use **of**, **off**, **does** and **goes** in these sentences. Write the correct word in each space.

One _____ the boys _____ not know the way back.

She jumped _____ the bed quickly.

Each day he _____ to see his grandma.

Which one _____ you knocked my tea _____ the table?

_____ anyone have a book to lend me?

Name

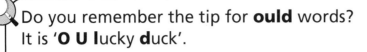**Objective:** Spell *ould* words.

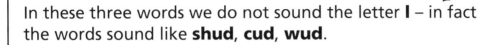
Supplementary unit **23** See Unit 18 **page 68**

Lucky duck

Do you remember the tip for **ould** words?
It is 'O U lucky duck'.

should   **could**   **would**

In these three words we do not sound the letter **l** – in fact
the words sound like **shud**, **cud**, **wud**.

Some more **ould** words are: **boulder**   **mouldy**   **shoulder**

In these three words the **l** is sounded (but the spellings are
still tricky!)

1. Write the correct **ould** word in these sentences.

I _____ not get into the cave because a large

_____ blocked the way.

You _____ not eat your chips with your fingers!

They cannot eat this bread – it is old and _____.

He hurt his _____ when he jumped off the wall.

W_____ you please help me to open this door?

2. Write two sentences of your own, using **ould** words.

_____

_____

_____

3. Put any new spellings in your wordbank.

Name

Piece of cake!

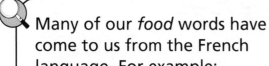

Many of our *food* words have come to us from the French language. For example: **restaurant**, **café** and **menu**.

Other words include: **gateau** (sounds like **gatoh**), **glacé** (sounds like **glasay**), **meringue** (sounds like **merang**) and **chef** (sounds like **shef**).

1. Use a dictionary to find out the meanings of **gateau**, **glacé**, **meringue** and **chef** and use them to complete these sentences. Add the new words to your wordbank.

The chocolate _____ with the fudge icing tasted superb.

I did not have enough egg whites to make a _____.

Dad put _____ cherries in the Christmas cake.

Everyone told the _____ what a good dinner it was.

2. Find out the meaning of **chateau** (sounds like **shatoh**). Its final five letters are exactly the same as in **gateau** – but it is not a food.

_____

3. Now write a sentence of your own, using **chateau**.

_____

_____

Name

Objective: Add *y* to nouns to make adjectives.

(**Supplementary unit** 25) See Unit 19 **pages 70–1**

A sunny day

1. Look at these pairs of words.

> sun – sunny   pen – penny
>
> bag – baggy   tum – tummy   pig – piggy

We double the last consonant before adding **y** in words like **sun** because the last three letters are consonant–vowel–consonant.

2. Add **y** to these words. Write the complete words.

cat _____   nut _____

fat _____   bug _____

rat _____   wit _____

(Check the meaning of any words you don't know.)

3. Finish these sentences.

I like going to the beach on a sun_____ day.

I bought a wool_____ coat.

His shoes were mud_____ after the walk.

The jelly was run_____.

4. Write the **y** words here.

_____   _____   _____   _____

Name

Objective: Spell plurals of words ending in f.

Supplementary unit **26** See Unit 19 **page 71**

Red roofs

Some words ending in **f** change the **f** to **v** and add **es** when they are plural, for example **loaf** – **loaves**.

Watch out for **roofs**, **chiefs**, **dwarfs** – they just end in **s**.

1. Write the correct plural word in these sentences.

My sister bought four (loaf) _____ for the picnic.

There were many (leaf) _____ on the ground after the high winds.

The seven (dwarf) _____ shared a large piece of gateau at teatime.

Some (thief) _____ came and stole her money.

The (roof) _____ on the houses were made of red tiles.

2. Write a sentence of your own, using the plural of **hoof**.

_____

_____

Name

Supplementary unit **27** See Unit 20 **pages 72–3**

Flying high

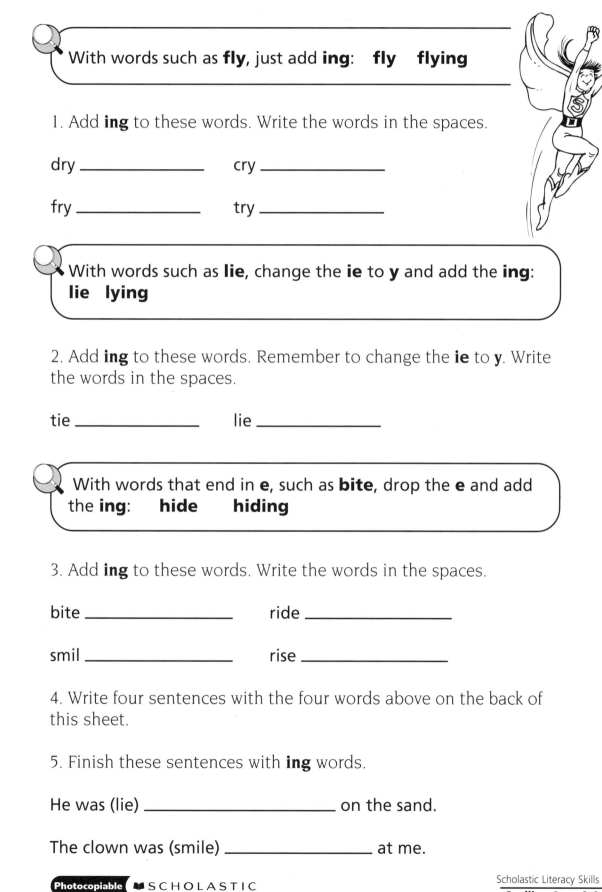

With words such as **fly**, just add **ing**: **fly   flying**

1. Add **ing** to these words. Write the words in the spaces.

dry _____   cry _____

fry _____   try _____

With words such as **lie**, change the **ie** to **y** and add the **ing**: **lie   lying**

2. Add **ing** to these words. Remember to change the **ie** to **y**. Write the words in the spaces.

tie _____   lie _____

With words that end in **e**, such as **bite**, drop the **e** and add the **ing**:   **hide   hiding**

3. Add **ing** to these words. Write the words in the spaces.

bite _____   ride _____

smil _____   rise _____

4. Write four sentences with the four words above on the back of this sheet.

5. Finish these sentences with **ing** words.

He was (lie) _____ on the sand.

The clown was (smile) _____ at me.

Name _____

Supplementary unit 28 See Unit 20 **pages 72–3**

Spy, spied, spying

1. Look at these words and say them aloud.

spy	spied	spying

Note what happens when the suffix **ed** is added. The **y** changes to **i**, but when **ing** is added, the **y** remains as it is.

2. Write the correct form of the words in brackets in the spaces.

She (pity) _____ the children who had no food to eat.

They watched me every day. I don't like them (spy)

_____ on me.

He is (hurry) _____ to catch his bus.

The grocer (supply) _____ them with food.

She never (reply) _____ to my letter.

"Wake up!" she (cry) _____.

The prince (marry) _____
Cinderella and they lived happily
ever after.

She was (try) _____ to cook
a meal, but the telephone kept
ringing.

Supplementary unit **29** **See Unit 20 page 73**

'ie' or 'ei'?

In many, but not all, **ie/ei** words, the **i** comes before the **e**. However, after the letter **c**, we nearly always put **e** before **i**.

Some other, common, words which have **e** before the **i** (and do not follow a letter **c**) are: **their**, **Keith**, **Sheila**, **weight**, **height**.

1. Read the following sentences aloud and write **ie** or **ei** in the spaces.

I saw my fr_____nd on Friday.

Is that th_____r dog?

There were many cows in the f_____ld.

Have a p_____ce of p_____.

Did K_____th rec_____ve my letter?

I trusted her, but she dec_____ved me.

A th_____f has taken my purse.

He looked down at the floor, then up at the c_____ling.

2. Now write two sentences of your own, using the words **weight** and **brief**.

_____

_____

Name

Sailing and surfing

1. Say these sports words in syllables.

sail ing

surf ing

2. Listen to the syllables. Write the full words.

_____   _____

When you add **ing** to some words, they *double* the last letter.

swim	skip	run	jog
swi**mm**ing	ski**pp**ing	ru**nn**ing	jo**gg**ing

3. Say the **ing** words. Write them in the spaces.

swimming

skipping

running

jogging

_____

_____

_____

_____

4. Use these four words in sentences of your own. Write them on the back of this sheet.

Name

Sporting story

1. Finish this sporting story. Fill in all the gaps.

I like holidays. I can play ten_____, net_____ and

crick_____. When we camp at the beach, I can go

surf_____ and swim_____ every day. Sometimes my dad

takes us hik_____ or sail_____ on the lake.

2. Add **ing** to these words. Write them in the tennis ball.

| swim | dive | jog | skate | run | dance | hike | surf |

Name

Supplementary unit 32 See Unit 22 **page 78**

Top of the league

Remember that **ue** is not sounded in the words **league** and **tongue**.

However the **ue** sounds like the **long vowel u** in words such as **cue**, **barbecue**, **argue**, **tissue** and **due**.

1. Write the correct **ue** word from the ones above in these sentences. Put any new **ue** words in your wordbank. Don't just copy!

I am _____ to see the dentist soon.

Their football team is top of the _____.

If the weather is good, we will have a _____.

Please don't _____ with me, I know I am right!

He stuck his _____ out at me.

Use a _____ if your nose runs, please.

I have my own snooker _____.

Name

Supplementary unit **33** See Unit 23 **page 80**

Clippety-clop

Clippety-clop

When I ride my black mare
She goes clippety-clop.
On paths and bush tracks
It is clippety-clop.
And up a steep slope,
Till she reaches the top.
Then off down the hillside
With clippety-clop.
Clippety, clippety, clippety-clop.

She crosses a stream
With a slip and a slop.
And off like a flash
With a clippety-clop.
She gallops so fast
That my ears start to pop.
Then back to our farm
Where she slides to a stop.
Clippety, clippety, clippety-clop.

Gordon Winch

1. Read this poem aloud. If you can, make it sound like a horse galloping. Listen to the consonants with **l** words.

2. Put circles around the two consonants that start the words. The first one has been done for you.

3. Write the three lines you like best here.

_____

_____

_____

Objective: Spell words with *silent b* and *silent k*.

Supplementary unit **34** See Unit 23 **pages 80–1**

Shhh!

We do not sound the last letter **b** in these words:

bom**b**   tom**b**   clim**b**   com**b**   crum**b**   thum**b**

Note: In the sentence **The soldiers were bombarded with bombs**, we sound the second letter **b** in **bombarded**. This may help you to remember the spelling of **bomb**.

1. Write the correct word in these sentences.

We are going to _____ the hill.

I have lost my _____ so my hair looks a mess!

There were many _____s on the floor after we had our tea.

I banged my _____ with the hammer.

The dead king was buried in a _____.

I was afraid when I heard _____s dropping.

2. Underline all the **silent k** words in these sentences. Say them aloud and write any new ones in your wordbank.

I know his mother knits every day.

They knew we were kneeling down.

The knight was fighting the dragon.

Name

Its or it's?

It's means **it is** (or **it has**). We put in the apostrophe to show that something has been left out. So always 'test' **its** by seeing if you can split it into two words – if you can't, do not put an apostrophe.

Its (without an apostrophe) means that something belongs to **it**.

1. Write **it's** or **its** in these sentences.

Sanjey is looking after the cat. I_____ fur is lovely and shiny

and i_____ nose has a little black dot on it.

I was reading a book, but i_____ cover has been lost.

I_____ a shame that he didn't score a goal.

The horse was eating hay from i_____ nosebag.

If i_____ a fine day, we will play tennis.

I saw the bird. I_____ wing was broken.

2. Write two sentences of your own, one using **its**, the other **it's**.

_____

_____

Name

Supplementary unit **36** See Unit 25 **page 84**

There, their and theirs

Remember that **their** and **theirs** are words about people or things belonging to them:

their ball   **their** team   those hiking books are **theirs**

1. Read these sentences. Write in the correct word (**there**, **their**, **theirs**).

Th_____ T-shirts need washing.

I think th_____ are some players missing.

If you see th_____ coach, tell me.

My favourite sport is swimming, but th_____ is running.

They took sandwiches for th_____ lunch.

Th_____ is no room left in the locker for all

th_____ trainers.

Name

Put them in order

1. Try to see how quickly you can find the names of these clothes in the dictionary. You can work with a partner and take it in turns to time each other.

trousers	jacket	dress	blouse	shirt
hat	coat	scarf	jumper	socks

2. Now put the words in alphabetical order

1. _____   6. _____

2. _____   7. _____

3. _____   8. _____

4. _____   9. _____

5. _____   10. _____

3. The words below are not spelled correctly. Check them in your dictionary. Put the correct spelling at the side.

rigt   _____   coton   _____

gowing _____   swiming _____

beleeve _____   ise cream _____

Name

What do they wear?

1. Look at the people above. Write their names in the boxes under each one. Choose from **boy**, **knight**, **princess** and **cowboy**.

2. What clothes are they wearing? Write the correct words on the labels. Pick from the words in the clothes basket.

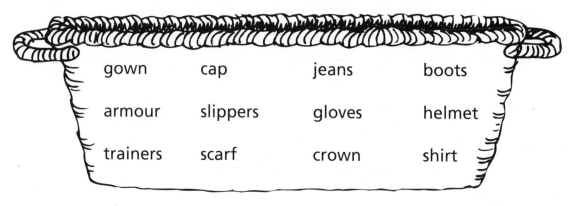

gown	cap	jeans	boots
armour	slippers	gloves	helmet
trainers	scarf	crown	shirt

3. Write any new words in your wordbank.

4. Which clothes would you like to wear? Why?

Name

Phantom Philip

1. Write words ending in the consonant blend **nd** in the spaces.

 The **consonant blend nd** is found at the end of some words, for example **blend**.

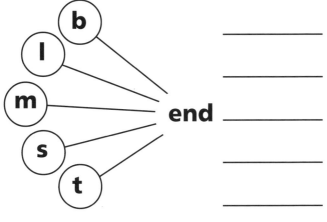

_____

_____

end _____

_____

_____

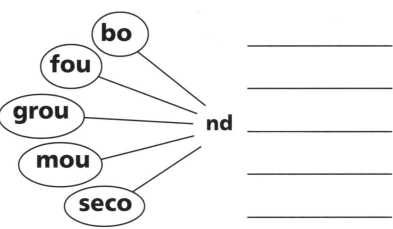

_____

_____

nd _____

_____

_____

2. Read these **ph** words and underline the **ph** in each. Write any new ones in your wordbank.

 ph is a digraph which sounds like **f**, as in **Philip**.

| photo | elephant | phantom | dolphin |
| telephone | orphan | telegraph | alphabet |

3. Write sentences for three of the words on the back of this sheet.

Name

Supplementary unit **40** See Unit 28 **pages 92–3**

The silent 'w'

1. Say these words beginning with a **silent w** aloud. Write them in your wordbank, then use them to fill the spaces in the sentences.

wrist	write	writing	wren	wreck
wrestle	wrap	wrapped	wring	wrong

I will _____ a letter on Wednesday.

Are you _____ your name on each piece of work?

He said my sums were all _____.

My swimming costume is wet. I will have to _____ it out.

The _____ is a very small bird.

The two men went into the ring and began to _____ each other.

He saw the _____ of the ship after the storm.

Have you _____ up my present?

He hurt his _____ when playing tennis.

I shall _____ my scarf round my neck.

Supplementary unit 41 See Unit 29 **page 95**

Special words

 Remember that the **ci** in the word spe**ci**al sounds like **sh**.

1. Here are some other **ci** words. Say the words aloud and then underline the **ci** in each one.

special   facial   precious   delicious   spacious   suspicious

2. Use the words in the sentences below.

The little baby is very

_____ to its mother.

Someone had eaten my chocolate. I was

_____ of my brother.

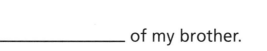

The lady used some _____ cream to make her skin smoother.

We had a lovely meal. It was _____.

Tomorrow is a _____ day. It is my birthday.

The room was very large. My dad said it was _____.

3. Now write a sentence of your own, using one of the **ci** words.

_____

_____

_____

Name _____

Supplementary unit **42** See Unit 30 **page 97**

Lawyers and doctors

A **trainer** is a rubber shoe for sport and also a person who trains people, usually for sports such as football or netball.

Many words used for people's jobs end in **er**. Some sound as though they end in **er**, but they end in **or**.

1. Read the words below, then write them in the correct **er** or **or** list. Write any new ones in your wordbank.

teacher	doctor	farmer	professor	mayor
instructor	grocer	painter	lawyer	tutor

or

_____

_____

_____

_____

er

_____

_____

_____

_____

2. Use some of the words to complete these sentences.

Her swimming _____ told her to see her _____ about the cramp she had.

The _____ wore a gold chain around his neck.

The _____ went to court nearly every day.

The _____ sold his vegetables to the green _____.